Cambridge Elements

Elements in the Psychology of Religion
edited by
Jonathan Lewis-Jong
St Mary's University Twickenham and University of Oxford

ATTACHMENT, RELIGION, AND SPIRITUALITY

Edward (Ward) B. Davis
Wheaton College (Illinois)

Pehr Granqvist
Stockholm University

Shaftesbury Road, Cambridge CB2 8EA, United Kingdom

One Liberty Plaza, 20th Floor, New York, NY 10006, USA

477 Williamstown Road, Port Melbourne, VIC 3207, Australia

314–321, 3rd Floor, Plot 3, Splendor Forum, Jasola District Centre, New Delhi – 110025, India

Cambridge University Press is part of Cambridge University Press & Assessment, a department of the University of Cambridge.

We share the University's mission to contribute to society through the pursuit of education, learning and research at the highest international levels of excellence.

www.cambridge.org
Information on this title: www.cambridge.org/9781009501033
DOI: 10.1017/9781009501019

© Edward (Ward) B. Davis and Pehr Granqvist 2026

This publication is in copyright. Subject to statutory exception and to the provisions of relevant collective licensing agreements, no reproduction of any part may take place without the written permission of Cambridge University Press & Assessment.

When citing this work, please include a reference to the DOI 10.1017/9781009501019

First published 2026

A catalogue record for this publication is available from the British Library

A Cataloging-in-Publication data record for this Element is available from the Library of Congress

ISBN 978-1-009-50103-3 Hardback
ISBN 978-1-009-50104-0 Paperback
ISSN 2753-6866 (online)
ISSN 2753-6858 (print)

Additional resources for this publication at www.cambridge.org/davis-granqvist.

Cambridge University Press & Assessment has no responsibility for the persistence or accuracy of URLs for external or third-party internet websites referred to in this publication and does not guarantee that any content on such websites is, or will remain, accurate or appropriate.

For EU product safety concerns, contact us at Calle de José Abascal, 56, 1°, 28003 Madrid, Spain, or email eugpsr@cambridge.org

Attachment, Religion, and Spirituality

Elements in the Psychology of Religion

DOI: 10.1017/9781009501019
First published online: March 2026

Edward (Ward) B. Davis
Wheaton College (Illinois)

Pehr Granqvist
Stockholm University

Author for correspondence: Edward (Ward) B. Davis,
ward.davis@wheaton.edu

Abstract: Across the world, most people are religious or spiritual, and many have a strong relational-emotional bond (attachment relationship) with God(s). This Element summarizes social-scientific theory and research on these relationships. Part I outlines basic principles of attachment and religion/spirituality. Part II describes normative (human-universal) processes and patterns. It explains how God and other supernatural beings often serve as irreplaceable relational caregivers (attachment figures), safe havens, and secure bases for people. Then it examines how religious/spiritual development interacts with attachment maturation across the lifespan. Part III explores individual differences in human and religious/spiritual attachment. After describing human-attachment differences, it examines how such differences can manifest jointly in forms of emotionally/socially correspondent or emotionally compensatory human attachment and religion/spirituality. Part IV discusses applied theory and research on religious/spiritual attachment. It explores the relationship between religious/spiritual attachment and health/well-being and concludes discussing how transformation in religious/spiritual attachment can occur through psychospiritual intervention or healthy relationships.

Keywords: attachment, religion, spirituality, relationships, psychology

© Edward (Ward) B. Davis and Pehr Granqvist 2026

ISBNs: 9781009501033 (HB), 9781009501040 (PB), 9781009501019 (OC)
ISSNs: 2753-6866 (online), 2753-6858 (print)

Contents

Part I   Conceptual Foundations of Attachment, Religion, and Spirituality   1

1 Attachment and Religion/Spirituality: Basic Concepts and Principles   1

Part II   Normative Patterns and Processes of Attachment and Religion/Spirituality   8

2 God and Other Supernatural Attachment Figures   8

3 Religious/Spiritual Development and Attachment Maturation   15

Part III   Individual Differences in Forms and Processes of Attachment and Religion/Spirituality   27

4 Individual Differences in Human Attachment   28

5 The Correspondence Facets of Human Attachment and Religion/Spirituality   43

6 The Compensation Facet of Human Attachment and Religion/Spirituality   55

Part IV   Applied Theory and Research on Religious/Spiritual Attachment   65

7 Religious/Spiritual Attachment, Health/Well-Being, and Transformation   65

References   79

Supplementary materials for this Element are available online at www.cambridge.org/davis-granqvist

Part I Conceptual Foundations of Attachment, Religion, and Spirituality

1 Attachment and Religion/Spirituality: Basic Concepts and Principles

I regard the desire to be loved and cared for as being an integral part of human nature.
John Bowlby (1979/2005, p. 184)

If you asked people what matters most in their life, most would say their close relationships with family and friends. Many would mention relationships with sacred beings such as God, Allah, or other deities. The most well-researched scientific theory of close relationships is attachment theory (Bowlby, 1969/1982, 1973, 1980; Cassidy & Shaver, 2016), and its application in the realm of people's religion/spirituality is called religious/spiritual (R/S) attachment theory (Granqvist, 2020) – the focus of this Element.

Part I of this Element summarizes basic concepts and principles of attachment and religion/spirituality (Section 1). Part II describes normative (human-universal) processes and patterns of attachment and religion/spirituality. We explain how God and other supernatural beings often serve as irreplaceable relational caregivers (*attachment figures*), safe havens, and secure bases for people (Section 2). We then discuss R/S development and its interaction with attachment maturation across the lifespan (Section 3). Next, we explore individual differences in the processes and forms of people's attachment and religion/spirituality (Part III). We describe these differences in terms of human attachment (Section 4) and examine how such differences can manifest jointly in forms of emotionally/socially correspondent (Section 5) or emotionally compensatory (Section 6) human attachment and religion/spirituality. Last, we discuss applied theory and research on R/S attachment (Part IV, Section 7), examining connections between R/S attachment and health/well-being, as well as how transformation in R/S attachment might occur. Throughout the Element, we will focus heavily on empirical research that has studied the relationship between R/S and attachment. Given space constraints, our inclusion of research studies had to be selective, but we have aspired to include as many high-quality and diverse (culturally, religiously/spiritually, and methodologically) studies as was reasonably possible.[1]

---

[1] Peer-reviewed empirical studies were identified through a PsycINFO database search, using the search string "TI (attachment AND ((religio* or spiritual* or faith or God))) OR AB (attachment AND ((religio* or spiritual* or faith or God)))" and the limiters *peer-reviewed*, *English language*, and *empirical study*. From this corpus of around 650 articles, we meticulously screened the titles and abstracts of all studies to narrow the corpus to only those that had central or peripheral relevance to this Element's topical focus. Those articles were then coded for various features (methodology, sample, setting, etc.). The full spreadsheet is available at https://osf.io/dmfz3/overview. Ultimately, we cited 113 of the 253 studies in this Element.

1.1 Basic Concepts in Attachment and Religion/Spirituality

Religion and spirituality have been defined countless ways. We define *spirituality* as people's search for and response to meaning and connection with whatever they perceive as sacred, including supernatural entities or aspects of life viewed either as a manifestation of the divine or as having transcendent or divine-like qualities. *Religion* refers more narrowly to people's search for and response to sacred meaning and connection in the context of culturally sanctioned codifications, rituals, and institutions. Considering how intertwined these phenomena are, we use *religion/spirituality* to refer collectively to people's search for and response to sacred meaning and connection (Davis et al., 2023).

An *attachment* is an enduring, strong emotional bond between two or more perceived living beings. Attachment bonds typically exhibit the following defining features. First, this bond develops and evolves through relational interactions and is persistent across time and situations. Second, at least one figure (an *attachment figure*) is perceived as holding irreplaceable emotional significance. Third, this figure's closeness and proximity are sought, especially during times of threat or distress. Fourth, their closeness and proximity are sought because this figure is expected to meet the attached individual's basic physical and psychological needs for safety, care, and security. Fifth, this figure optimally functions as a source of protection, care, and comfort (*safe haven*) during times of threat or distress and a source of emotional strength and security (*secure base*) during novel or challenging situations. Sixth, physical or emotional separation from this figure leads the attached individual to experience distress, and the actual/perceived loss of the figure leads that individual to experience grief (Ainsworth, 1989; Bowlby, 1969/1982, 1973, 1980).

1.2 Basic Principles and Hypotheses of Attachment Theory

This Element focuses on R/S attachment, but first we summarize the basic principles/hypotheses of attachment theory more generally. We have adapted the list that Simpson et al. (2021) synthesized in consultation with attachment experts. Besides slightly revising and expanding their list, we have reorganized it into two sections – principles of normative attachment processes/patterns (Principles 1–5) and principles of individual differences in attachment forms/processes (Principles 6–10).

1.2.1 Basic Principles of Normative Attachment Patterns and Processes

Principle 1: Attachment theory is an evolutionary and biologically based theory. It is built on the assumption that humans (and certain other animals such as birds, rodents, dogs/wolves, and nonhuman primates) have a genetically programmed predisposition to seek proximity to caregivers important for their safety and survival.

1a: All humans engage in this proximity-seeking behavior to meet their basic physical and psychological needs (*universality hypothesis*).

1b: The strong, enduring emotional bond that develops with an irreplaceable caregiver whose proximity is sought during times of threat or distress is an *attachment*.

1c: The irreplaceable caregivers who meet these needs are *attachment figures* (Simpson et al., 2021).

Principle 2: Humans (and certain other animals) are born with innate psychobiological systems that guide perceptions and interactions with their social surroundings. These include the attachment, caregiving, exploration, affiliation, and sexual behavioral systems.

2a: These psychobiological systems of social behavior are interrelated and important for physical survival, environmental adaptation, and genetic reproduction.

2b: Each system has an evolved mental/neural program that motivates behavioral strategies for attaining certain goal states that optimize chances for survival and reproduction. These strategies are mentally/neurally activated by stimuli or situations that make the desired goal state salient. They are deactivated/terminated by other stimuli or outcomes that signal the desired goal state has been attained.

2c: The attachment behavioral system becomes mentally/neurally activated during situations of perceived threat (*threat activation hypothesis*), namely circumstances of distress, fear, pain, fatigue, sickness, separation, or loss. In these situations, the elicited primary behavioral strategy is proximity seeking to actual, perceived, or internalized attachment figures (Mikulincer & Shaver, 2016; Simpson et al., 2021).

Principle 3: Actual/perceived separation from an attachment figure leads to distress, and the actual/perceived loss of an attachment figure leads to grief.

3a: There are three phases characterizing the typical response to separation from or loss of an attachment figure: protest, despair, and detachment/reorganization.

3b: Each phase serves an evolutionarily adaptive function. Protest helps draw back the caregiver's attention, care, and proximity. Despair helps downregulate the attached individual's emotional/behavioral distress when protest is unsuccessful. Detachment/reorganization helps the person move on without the caregiver, develop new internal capacities (for self-regulation/self-reliance), and form bonds with potential new caregivers (Cassidy & Shaver, 2016; Simpson et al., 2021).

Principle 4: Attachment relationships ideally serve three core psychophysiological functions – supporting proximity seeking/maintenance, offering a safe haven, and providing a secure base. Each function facilitates the attached individual's self-regulation capacities (abilities to control and direct their biopsychosocial–R/S responses).

4a: The proximity seeking/maintenance function helps support their safety and survival through gaining/maintaining physical or emotional closeness to real, perceived, or internalized attachment figures. This closeness contributes to a psychophysiological sense of feeling safe, calm, cared for, and confident (*felt security*).

4b: The safe haven function operates when the attachment figure offers protection, care, or comfort during times of real or perceived threat/distress. This function meets basic psychophysiological needs for safety, predictability, and care.

4c: The secure base function operates when the attachment figure provides a sense of confidence to explore surroundings and to face challenging or novel situations. This function meets basic psychological needs for competence, autonomy, and growth. Over time it leads to improved self-regulation and optimal biopsychosocial–R/S development (Cassidy & Shaver, 2016; Mikulincer & Shaver, 2016; Simpson et al., 2021).

Principle 5: Experiences in attachment relationships shape the development of malleable mental/neural representations of oneself, others, and the world (called *internal working models*; IWMs).

5a: These mental/neural representations are cognitive/affective structures and neural firing patterns formed from encoded implicit (often-nonconscious) and explicit (consciously available) memories of interactions with one's physical and social environment.

5b: As generalized memories of experiences, these representations guide perceptions, expectations, and biopsychosocial–R/S responses toward oneself, others, and the world.

5c: These experience-based representations shape how the individual responds to attachment threat and how they perceive and interact with themselves, others, and the world. In other words, these mental/neural representations underlie the attachment dispositions/habits an individual develops (Davis et al., 2021; Simpson et al., 2021; cf. Vannucci et al., 2025).

1.2.2 Basic Principles of Individual Differences in Attachment Forms and Processes

Principle 6: Individual differences in attachment dispositions/habits are prototypically reflected in a particular response to attachment threat/distress and to an underlying constellation of mental/neural representations of oneself, others, and the world.

6a: A secure attachment disposition is prototypically reflected in a proximity-seeking response to threat/distress and in representations of oneself as lovable and capable, others as available and responsive, and the world as safe and predictable.

6b: An insecure–avoidant/dismissing attachment disposition is prototypically reflected in an emotion-deactivating response to threat/distress and in representations of oneself as alone but capable, others as unavailable and unresponsive, and the world as uninterested and uninteresting.

6c: An insecure–resistant/preoccupied attachment disposition is prototypically reflected in an emotion-hyperactivating response to threat/distress and in representations of oneself as unlovable and incapable, others as inconsistently available and responsive, and the world as variably safe and predictable.

6d: Disorganized–disoriented/unresolved attachment is prototypically reflected in a chaotic/incoherent response to threat/distress and in representations of the world as unpredictable or terrifying and of oneself and others as frightened, frightening, or fragmented (Cassidy & Shaver, 2016; Mikulincer & Shaver, 2016; Simpson et al., 2021).

Principle 7: The quality of the relational connection between an infant/child's attachment system and their early caregiver's caregiving system is what determines the attachment-relevant mental/neural representations the infant/child initially develops. Hence, it determines how secure versus insecure (and/or disorganized–disoriented) the infant/child's early attachment is.

7a: Early caregiving that is consistently available, caring, and sensitive, especially during times of threat/distress, contributes to the infant/child experiencing attachment security and initially developing a principal secure attachment disposition (*caregiving sensitivity hypothesis*).

7b: Early caregiving that is inconsistently available, caring, or sensitive, especially during times of threat/distress, contributes to the infant/child experiencing attachment insecurity and initially developing a principal insecure (resistant or avoidant) attachment disposition.

7c: Early caregiving that is sufficiently frightening or anomalous, especially during times of threat/distress, can lead the infant/child to experience attachment disorientation and develop a habitual response of disorganized–disoriented attachment (Cassidy & Shaver, 2016; Mikulincer & Shaver, 2016; Simpson et al., 2021).

Principle 8: The attachment behavioral system is active throughout the lifespan. Across development, expression of attachment-related needs moves from concrete physical, help-seeking behaviors during infancy/toddlerhood toward internalized, representational processes (e.g., talking with or thinking about attachment figures) from preschool age onward. Attachment targets also change, usually shifting from caregivers during early/middle childhood to close friends and romantic partners from adolescence onward. Because of cognitive maturations associated with symbolic thinking and mentalization, young people become increasingly capable of imagining and directing attachment-related behaviors and mental processes toward noncorporeal attachment figures such as God(s) (Granqvist, 2020).

8a: Over the lifespan, attachment dispositions/habits are somewhat stable across time, situations, and contexts, especially when it comes to a principal secure attachment disposition (*attachment stability hypothesis*).

8b: Early attachments have a disproportionate effect on subsequent attachments, because early life is a sensitive period for attachment development.

8c: Nevertheless, the possibility of attachment-related change remains open throughout the lifespan. Yet, as humans age, change may happen more slowly, require more effort, or be more unlikely altogether.

8d: At whatever life phase, attachment dispositions/habits (and the mental/neural representations underlying them) can change based on new attachment-relevant experiences (*attachment change hypothesis*). Such change is particularly likely when new attachment-relevant experiences sharply and persistently contradict previous ones (Mikulincer & Shaver, 2016, 2023a, 2023b; Simpson et al., 2021; cf. Vannucci et al., 2025).

Principle 9: A secure attachment disposition is an experience-accrued, inner, psychophysiological–R/S resource that often supports optimal biopsychosocial–R/S development and functioning (*broaden-and-build hypothesis of attachment security*). Insecure and disorganized attachments are experience-accrued, inner, psychophysiological–R/S vulnerabilities that can impede optimal biopsychosocial–R/S development and functioning (*vulnerability hypothesis of attachment insecurity/disorganization*).

9a: A secure attachment disposition often promotes positive psychophysiological health (mental and physical health/well-being). When contrasted with secure attachment, insecure or disorganized attachment can contribute to negative psychophysiological health and functioning (mental or physical illness/dysfunction).

9b: A secure attachment disposition often promotes positive social health outcomes, such as close, caring, and stable relationships. Insecure or disorganized attachment can contribute to negative social health outcomes, including interpersonal difficulties and dysfunction like distant, uncaring, unstable, traumatizing, or abusive relationships (Cassidy & Shaver, 2016; Mikulincer & Shaver, 2016; Simpson et al., 2021).

9c: A secure attachment disposition often promotes positive R/S health outcomes like R/S maturity, whereas insecure or disorganized attachment can contribute to negative R/S health outcomes like R/S struggles (Davis et al., 2021, 2023; Pargament & Exline, 2022).

Principle 10: Although the attachment behavioral system is human-universal, it is also culturally dependent and can result in culturally variable forms of biopsychosocial–R/S development and adaptation.

10a: In some cultural groups/contexts, most individuals develop a principal secure attachment disposition (*normativity hypothesis*). This cultural pattern may emerge because people in these groups/contexts are exposed to relatively higher rates of high-quality attachment relationships (sensitive, responsive caregiving) and environmental conditions (nonthreatening, well-resourced contexts).

10b: In other cultural groups/contexts, comparatively more individuals develop principal insecure and/or disorganized attachment. This cultural pattern may emerge because people in these groups/contexts are exposed to relatively higher rates of poor-quality attachment relationships (insensitive, less-responsive, or traumatizing caregiving) or environmental conditions (threatening or under-resourced contexts; Cassidy & Shaver, 2016; Simpson et al., 2021; Thompson et al., 2021).

1.3 Conclusion

These basic principles form the foundation for our discussion of normative patterns/processes in Part II and individual differences in attachment forms/processes in Part III. Throughout this Element, we periodically use case examples to illustrate these principles. All cases are from the lives of famous figures and based on psychospiritual analysis of (auto)biographical or other primary sources. These examples will bring the principles of attachment to life and show how central attachment is to human life and religion/spirituality.

Nevertheless, we urge readers to recognize that the veracity of these basic principles rests on research and theorizing at the group-level (which is termed "nomothetic" science). This type of science deals with general principles and metrics, like averages/means and correlations (e.g., correlations between caregiver sensitivity and child attachment security). Although there is robust empirical support for these principles, the effect sizes of these findings are often small-to-moderate, like in psychological science more generally. This fact implies there will be many individuals for whom some general principles do not apply (e.g., some people develop a secure attachment disposition despite receiving relatively insensitive caregiving). This caveat is especially important to consider when understanding particular individuals ("idiographic" science), such as this Element's case examples. People, their attachments, and their religion/spirituality are highly dynamic and complex, as are the socioecological contexts in which they live and develop.

Part II Normative Patterns and Processes of Attachment and Religion/Spirituality

Within the social sciences, attachment theory and research are unusual in their focus both on species-typical considerations ("normative" patterns/processes of attachment) and individual differences (in forms/processes of attachment). When it comes to religion/spirituality, humans also exhibit normative features of religion/spirituality (cross-culturally evident cognitive, emotional, moral, and social motivations/functions of religion/spirituality; Saroglou, 2011) and variegated individual differences in R/S habits (Davis et al., 2023).

Part II explores the normative features of attachment (Section 2) and developmental interactions between attachment and religion/spirituality (Section 3). It de-emphasizes individual differences and other sources of variation (cultural, societal, etc.) because those are the focus of Parts III and IV.

2 God and Other Supernatural Attachment Figures

"The greatest disease in the [world] today is not [tuberculosis] or leprosy; it is being unwanted, unloved, and uncared for. We can cure physical diseases with medicine, but the only cure for loneliness, despair, and hopelessness is love . . . . There's a hunger for love, as there is a hunger for God."

– Mother Teresa (1995, p. 79)

Imagine traveling worldwide and asking people to name the most positively influential figures in modern history. Perhaps they mention luminaries like

Mother Teresa, Mahatma Gandhi, Nelson Mandela, Billy Graham, Pope John Paul II, the Dalai Lama, Malala Yousafzai, Martin Luther King, Jr., or Abraham Lincoln. Though by no means flawless, each of these individuals helped bring incalculable love, good, and justice into the world.

But what if you could travel back and ask each luminary what helped *them* have such an impact? Most would mention their religion/spirituality, and many would point to their relationship with God(s). Why?

Section 2 explores answers to this and related questions like: Why are there so few atheists in foxholes or on their deathbeds? Why does every human heart hunger for love? Across history, why have humans yearned for a love so deep, constant, generous, and unconditional that it might seem to emanate from somewhere transcendent – beyond the horizons of frail humanity? Was Mother Teresa right? Is our universal hunger for love intertwined with a universal hunger for God(s)?

2.1 Humans' Relational Need and Drive for Surrogate Attachment Figures

As children enter and navigate middle childhood (~ages 6–12), they have usually developed attachment bonds with other figures besides their primary caregivers. These *surrogate attachment figures* can include siblings, other relatives (aunts/uncles, grandparents, etc.), and mentors (teachers/coaches). Likewise, adolescents and young adults typically form attachment bonds with peers and romantic partners, who in due course may become their principal attachment figures, supplanting parents as the main source of emotional safety, nurturance, and security. Teens and adults can also develop attachment bonds with mentors, clergy, coworkers, psychotherapists, and so forth (Ainsworth, 1989).

But each of these attachment figures, the primary caregivers of childhood included, has a fundamental limitation – they are human. And human attachment figures cannot know and do everything. They cannot be present everywhere, all the time. They will not always respond to or understand you perfectly. They will fail and make mistakes. Despite their good intentions, they sometimes will disappoint and hurt you. People are imperfect, relationships are messy, and humans are limited by time, space, and countless frailties. So where does that leave us? Let us look at two examples from history.

2.1.1 Frida Kahlo: Pets as Surrogate Attachment Figures

Frida Kahlo (1907–1954), one of the most famous Hispanic painters of all time, had a challenging, tumultuous life. The Mexican Revolution began when she was 3 years old, embroiling her community and nation in chaos and violence until she was 13. Additionally, at age 6, Frida contracted polio, leaving her bedridden for months and causing her to develop physical abnormalities and difficulties for which she was bullied. She also was in a terrible bus accident at age 18, resulting in severe injuries, lifelong pain, and the physical inability to have children. A few years later, she married Diego Rivera, another famous Mexican painter, but they had a volatile relationship marked by emotional chaos, serial infidelities, recurrent separations, and a divorce and quick remarriage. Frida lived through three other brutal wars – World War I (1914–1917), Spanish Civil War (1936–1939), and World War II (1939–1945) – and she and her husband were activists during the latter two (Herrera, 1983).

But not only was Frida's external world challenging and tumultuous, her internal world was as well. Perhaps because her relationships with each parent were so different, Frida seems to have developed complex, contradictory attachment representations and dispositions that guided how she navigated life. For example, she had a fiery, emotive, and creative personality, which did not mesh well with her stern, rigid, and restrictive mother (a hyper-religious Catholic woman of Spanish, indigenous-Mexican, and Asian-Indian descent). Frida seems to have developed an insecure–resistant/preoccupied attachment with her mother, marked by a mixture of love and contempt. Her mother cared well for Frida physically as a child, but they struggled to connect emotionally and had frequent, intense fights. Conversely, Frida always had a close, secure attachment with her father, a Hungarian-German man who grew up Jewish but became an avowed atheist and emigrated to Mexico in the 1890s. Frida's father had a quiet and warm but serious personality. Throughout Frida's life, he was caring, patient, and empowering. He cared for her physical/socioemotional needs and nurtured her resilience, rebelliousness, independence, and assertiveness, as well as her artistic and creative genius (Herrera, 1983).

Besides her father, what helped Frida cope with her challenging internal and external world? Certainly art was a major outlet for her, but Frida also developed many surrogate attachments – with her boisterous gaggle of pets. From early childhood, she was always surrounded by a beloved personal zoo that included a parrot, three dogs, a cat, two spider monkeys, an eagle, two turkeys, and a deer. She relied heavily on these pets for comfort, compassion, and companionship (Brown, 2017). She played with them daily and cared for them tenderly, perhaps having learned to care for them with the same sensitivity her father had always shown her. Frida's pets offered her a lifelong source of joy, confidence, and inspiration, appearing in 55 of her nearly 150 masterpieces, most of which were self-portraits (Esfandiari, 2025). They helped Frida care for, understand, and express herself in ways that inspire people worldwide.

2.1.2 Rumi: God(s) as Surrogate Attachment Figure(s)

Mohammad Jalâl al-Din Rumi (1207–1273), the famed Muslim poet, developed surrogate attachments another way. He was born in modern-day Tajikistan. When Rumi was 5 years old, his family began a 17-year, 2,500-mile migration, settling a few times along the way. During their journey, Rumi got married and had two sons, yet his mother died. Three years after Rumi settled permanently in Konya, modern-day Turkey, his father – an Islamic scholar and jurist with whom Rumi had a close and seemingly secure attachment – died as well. After his father's death in 1231, Rumi developed a surrogate attachment relationship with a spiritual/scholarly mentor who shaped Rumi's studies, spiritual life, and career but died in 1241. Rumi's wife died the following year, and he quickly remarried. Ultimately, a surrogate attachment relationship that started in 1244 transformed Rumi's soul and awakened his masterful poetry (Lewis, 2000).

For the next 4 years, Rumi and Shams al-Din Tabrizi became soulmates. Shams al-Din became a deified spiritual guide and friend. Rumi was transformed by the relational–spiritual experiences they shared. They experienced a deeper relational–spiritual union with God and each other than Rumi thought possible. The zeniths of elevation they shared are what inspired Rumi's first torrent of poetry (Lewis, 2000).

Unfortunately, some of Rumi's family and disciples were so jealous of this intense attachment that they drove Shams out of town. Rumi was so devastated and despairing that his disciples eventually apologized and helped find Shams and bring him back. Shams and Rumi enjoyed another year of relational–spiritual bliss, but in 1248, Shams disappeared again – this time for good. Another torrent of poetry deluged from Rumi, mourning the loss of his soulmate. After years of failed attempts to find Shams, Rumi announced having a revelation that he and Shams had spiritually merged: "Since I'm [Shams], for what do I search? I'm his mirror image and will speak myself" (Lewis, 2000, p. 288).

Rumi then redirected his intense attachment needs and energies to attaining perfect union with God. God became Rumi's supreme surrogate attachment figure. God was the consummate source and focus of Rumi's love for the remaining 25 years of Rumi's life (Lewis, 2000). Over the centuries, Rumi's poems have inspired inestimable souls searching for the echelons of divine, human, and self-actualized love that Rumi painted with words.

2.2 The Human Draw toward God and Other Surrogate Attachment Figures

Rumi and Frida chose different strategies for developing attachment relationships with nonhuman surrogate attachment figures – Frida with pets and Rumi with God. Naturally, neither strategy is inherently more health-promoting or psychologically beneficial than the other, but this Element focuses on the latter strategy – people who develop an attachment relationship with God(s).

The psychological appeal of an attachment relationship with God(s) is compelling. Most world religions/spiritualities espouse a belief that their deity, deities, or divine transcendent force is perfect in every way. Perfectly moral, faultless, wise, all-knowing, accessible, ever-present, benevolent, and so forth (Granqvist, 2020). Who would *not* want a relationship with that type of being/force?

Let us even try something as we consider this point. Think of the most loving and good person you have ever known. Remember a few cherished experiences you shared with them. Savor those fond memories a moment.

Now imagine someone who was transcendently even *more* loving and good than that person. Someone who was always accessible. Always knew your innermost thoughts, feelings, and longings. Always cared. Listened. Forgave. Had the perfect words and advice. Knew everything happening in your life – both inside and around you. Always had the most heartwarming, soul-inspiring way to respond. Always had your best in mind, even when you did not know what that was. What it would be like interacting with that being all the time? How might that feel? How could it shape your life? Your heart? Your health and well-being?

As you consider what you just experienced, it might make more sense why across millennia, world civilizations have practiced prosocial religions that involve perfectly powerful, benevolent, and knowing gods (Norenzayan et al., 2016). Some of these religions (like Buddhism, Hinduism, other East Asian religions, and many New Age spiritualities) have beliefs and practices centering on nonrelational gods or impersonal forces. Yet even in these religions, many adherents develop relationships with supernatural entities that function as surrogate attachment figures. This phenomenon is evident among followers of New Age spiritualities (Granqvist, 2020), Hinduism (attachment to God[s]; Fincham et al., 2019), and many other Asian-birthed faiths (attachment to nature and the universe in Daoism/Taoism, to a divine cosmic force in Zen Buddhism, and to divine and humanistic consciousness in Confucianism; Ai et al., 2013). It is also evident among the exponentially growing number of people who identify as Spiritual But Not Religious (Johnson et al., 2018).

Nevertheless, across history and cultures, the religions whose adherents have most prototypically developed R/S attachment relationships are Christianity (with God, Jesus, the Holy Spirit, Virgin Mary, and/or saints), Judaism (with G-d), and Islam (with Allah and the Prophet Muhammad). Within and across these Abrahamic faiths, there are abundant differences in beliefs, practices, sacred texts, and theologies. Yet each of these traditions espouse a core belief in a perfect God with whom adherents can – and should – have a relationship. They may not explicitly refer to such a relationship as an attachment relationship, but functionally, the relationship they prototypically prescribe is an attachment one (Granqvist, 2020).

2.3 The Believer–God Relationship Can Exhibit the Defining Features of an Attachment Bond

In Section 1, we described several defining features of attachment bonds. Attachment scholars Kirkpatrick, Shaver, and Granqvist have pioneered work discussing how people's perceived relationship with God often exhibits these defining features (Granqvist, 2020; Kirkpatrick & Shaver, 1990, 1992).

2.3.1 Religion/Spirituality as a Loving Relationship

The Abrahamic traditions – Judaism, Islam, and especially Christianity – are quite relational in their theology, such that a personal relationship with God is often central to their R/S beliefs and practices. Many theistic believers – particularly Protestant Christians – describe love as central to their relationship with God, akin to how they describe falling and staying in love with a romantic partner or being loved by a caring, security-enhancing parent (Granqvist & Kirkpatrick, 2016). Granqvist (2020) has even argued that religion/spirituality *is* an attachment for large portions of the global population.

2.3.2 God as Uniquely Irreplaceable

Additionally, a theistic believer's relationship with God is prototypically characterized by a sense of God's irreplaceable uniqueness. Even as Bowlby (1969/1982) described children regarding their attachment figures as stronger and wiser than themselves, theistic believers are normatively taught that God is the ultimate stronger and wiser One who alone is omnipotent (all-powerful – can do anything), omniscient (all-knowing – knows everything in the past, present, and future), omnipresent (all-present – is everywhere at all times), omnipure (all-holy – is without fault and incapable of R/S or moral wrongdoing), and omnibenevolent (all-good – has benevolent qualities and intentions that guide every thought, feeling, and action). Of course, every believer does not represent God mentally in these charitable ways (see Part III), but the Abrahamic faiths usually describe and approach God in ways that align with humans' deep-rooted yearning for ever-present love, safety, and security – in the form of a uniquely irreplaceable God.

2.3.3 Seeking and Maintaining Proximity to God

Because God is viewed as always available, benevolent, competent, and capable, theistic believers prototypically seek and maintain proximity to God, particularly during times of threat/distress. They seek and maintain this perceived closeness through R/S practices like prayer, worship, or other rituals that foster a sense of believer–God connectedness. Through this felt connectedness, God meets the believer's basic physical and psychological needs for safety, care, and comfort, restoring or enhancing a sense of felt security (Granqvist, 2020).

2.3.4 God as a Safe Haven

Religious and nonreligious people alike tend to turn to God(s) for protection, care, or comfort in situations that activate the attachment system, namely times of threat, distress, fear, pain, fatigue, sickness, separation, or loss. There is robust experimental evidence of this among adults (Birgegard & Granqvist, 2004; Granqvist et al., 2012b) and children (Granqvist et al., 2007b). Moreover, there is longitudinal evidence of it among people affected by major stressors like natural disasters (Davis et al., 2019), terrorist attacks (Peterson & Seligman, 2003), bereavement (Brown et al., 2004), and personal suffering (Granqvist, 2020).

2.3.5 God as a Secure Base

Another defining feature of an attachment bond is that the attachment figure offers a secure base for supporting confidence, exploration, play, and creativity. When God provides this sense of felt security, believers feel God is a secure base from which they can navigate new situations, take risks, build new skills, have fun, express creativity, and face challenges. For instance, in a series of seven studies, reminders of God increased people's likelihood of taking risks in nonmoral situations, especially if they already had a secure attachment relationship with God (Kupor et al., 2015). Similarly, in Cassibba et al.'s (2014) study of adults diagnosed with a serious disease, patients were most likely to exhibit a "fighting spirit" (p. 252) if they had a secure relationship with God. Patients with an insecure relationship with God tended to exhibit more hopelessness.

2.3.6 Responses to Perceived Separation or Loss

Another defining feature of an attachment bond is that the attached person experiences distress when separated from the attachment figure and grief following the actual/perceived loss of that figure. For theistic believers, this type of separation or loss can take the form of feeling a short-term sense of separation or distance/disconnectedness from God, especially if they are facing an already-distressing situation and are used to feeling God's closeness and comfort. Even as humans long for their close relationship figures to be there for them when it matters, when it feels like God is not there emotionally, believers can experience distress, frustration, or anger. If this perceived separation persists, then grief or compounded anger can result. Such responses can take on many forms, including a "dark night of the soul" (St. John of the Cross, 1953/2003), divine R/S struggles (anger/disappointment with God; Pargament & Exline, 2022), or even unresolved R/S trauma or loss (see Section 4's discussion of connections between unresolved trauma/loss and disorganized attachment; Granqvist, 2020).

2.4 Conclusion

Section 2 explored humans' relational need and drive for relationships with surrogate attachment figures (relational beings/forces besides their primary caregivers). These surrogate figures can include other people (friends, romantic partners, relatives, etc.), nonhuman animals (pets), or supernatural entities (God[s] and other sacred beings/forces). This chapter and Element focus on why people often develop an attachment relationship with God(s).

Across history, people have developed this type of R/S attachment relationship, especially adherents of Judaism, Christianity, and Islam. A considerable body of research evidence supports the idea that believer–God relationships can (and often do) exhibit the defining features of attachment relationships – God as irreplaceably unique, seeking/maintaining proximity to God, God as a safe haven and secure base, and responding to perceived separation from God with distress and to perceived lost closeness to God with grief (Granqvist, 2020).

Nevertheless, there are key differences between God and human attachment figures. Unlike God, human attachment figures are visible and audible, and attachment relationships with humans will have a history of potentially observable interactions. Yet rather than invalidating an attachment conceptualization of religion/spirituality, these and other differences may simply reflect artifacts of normative human cognitive development, some of which we explore next.

3 Religious/Spiritual Development and Attachment Maturation

> *"Whilst especially evident during early childhood, attachment behavior is held to characterize human beings from the cradle to the grave."*
> – John Bowlby (1979/2005, p. 154)

Section 2 focused on the attachment–R/S connection during adulthood, because we needed to describe how God often functions as a surrogate attachment figure for people across the lifespan. Section 3 explores each developmental phase in depth, discussing how R/S development and attachment maturation co-occur. We adopt a lifespan developmental–maturational approach and argue that people's broader attachment-related maturation undergirds the development and maturation of their R/S representations, dispositions, and experiences. Section 3 mostly describes R/S development from an attachment-maturation lens, organized by developmental phase, but before proceeding, we ground this discussion in some basic concepts and principles of development and maturation.

3.1 Basic Concepts and Principles of Development and Maturation

R/S development is the progressive series of changes in the structure, function, and response patterns that characterize people's search for and response to sacred meaning and connection (Davis et al., 2023). *Attachment development* is the progressive series of changes in the structure, function, and response patterns that characterize how people perceive and respond to attachment figures, regardless of whether those figures are same-species or other-species (e.g., pets), actual or perceived (e.g., noncorporeal), and human or supernatural (e.g., God[s]). *Attachment maturation* refers to the emergence of attachment-relevant biopsychosocial–R/S capacities that occur via species-typical growth processes (Granqvist, 2020).

All human development – including R/S and attachment development – unfolds as a complex interaction between nature (energy and information input from biological and genetic predispositions) and nurture (energy and information input from environmental factors and experiences). This fact of nature–nurture (gene–environment) interactions permeating development is now generally accepted by scientists, practitioners, and laypeople alike (Granqvist, 2020).

3.2 R/S Development vis-à-vis Attachment Maturation

This section explores how R/S development builds on attachment-related maturations that emerge during specific developmental periods. We discuss four key phases, recognizing these phases are not as discrete as they may seem: infancy/toddlerhood (~age 0–3 years), early childhood (~age 3–6), middle childhood (~age 6–12), adolescence and young adulthood (~age 12–30), and middle to older adulthood (~age 30 to death).

3.2.1 Infancy and Toddlerhood

During their first months, infants typically move through a preattachment phase (Bowlby, 1969/1982) in which they interact with others rather indiscriminately (smiling, babbling, etc.). They gradually exhibit increasing preference for familiar caregivers (those caregivers' voices, faces, and smells), relative to less-familiar people. It usually takes until age 6 or 7 months to form a full-fledged attachment relationship with their primary caregiver(s). Bowlby (1969/1982) described infants' first attachment to a primary caregiver as the key prototype from which their initial attachment representations and dispositions/habits develop.

Between 6 and 12 months, the infant shows an increasingly strong preference for their primary caregiver(s). They also exhibit increasing separation anxiety when away from their caregiver(s) and wariness over interacting with strangers. Separation anxiety and stranger wariness are universally evident, but across children and cultures, this anxiety and wariness can vary in intensity and expression (Bowlby, 1973). The infant actively turns to their caregiver(s) to function as a *safe haven* (source of comfort/protection) when distressed or threatened and as a *secure base* (source of confidence/competence) when facing new or difficult situations. As part of this maturation, infants use *social referencing* (seeking emotional, verbal, and gestural cues from their caregiver[s] to enhance a sense of confidence and competence). This referencing helps guide infants while they explore new physical and psychosocial terrains (Granqvist, 2020).

The second half of the first year is also marked by major increases in the infant's physical mobility (crawling and eventually walking) and cognitive development, such as the attainment of *object permanence* (the ability to recognize a person or thing continues existing even when it is not physically present/visible). Rudimentary *symbolization* (the ability to let one object, gesture, or idea stand for another) begins emerging as well (e.g., pointing toward a desired object). Moreover, the infant is growing rapidly in abilities to recognize and differentiate oneself from others, express one's needs and desires through language and gestures, and behave in ways that elicit attention and care from primary caregivers. They are starting to recognize symbols in their environment (e.g., a menorah) and may eventually form psychophysiological associations with those symbols (e.g., feelings of awe, joy, and love), laying the foundations for R/S representations if the infant is being raised in an R/S household, community, or culture (Granqvist, 2020).

The developmental window between age 6 and 36 months is perhaps the most impactful sensitive period of attachment in the human lifespan. The attachment bond(s), representations, and dispositions/habits formed during this time often have a disproportionately strong and long-lasting influence on how the developing child relates to themselves and others. There are, of course, ample opportunities for change during subsequent phases, but the formative, often-enduring influence of this sensitive period is noteworthy (Cozolino, 2024; Siegel, 2020). During this period, the infant–toddler's attachment system is frequently activated, visibly functioning, and rapidly developing, even as the child is rapidly developing physically, cognitively, linguistically, socially, and emotionally (Granqvist, 2020).

Regarding R/S development and attachment maturation, the infant–toddler period can be viewed as largely pre-R/S until around age 2. Infants and young toddlers are generally absorbed by their senses – how concrete objects and people smell, sound, look, feel, and taste. They may be generally unaware and uninterested in the invisible, nonphysical realms of religion/spirituality, especially if they have no or minimal R/S socialization in their family or surrounding culture. Ideally, the infant–toddler's main R/S developmental task is simply to bask in their caregivers' steadfast love, learning to trust attachment figures for practical and emotional comfort, care, and support. In so doing, the infant–toddler develops foundational psychological capacities that eventually enable them to trust other human (and potentially noncorporeal) attachment figures for comfort, care, and support (Fowler, 1987; Granqvist, 2020).

Because of their nascent cognitive and socioemotional capacities, infants and toddlers younger than 18 months usually do not have the psychological capacity to develop an attachment relationship with a noncorporeal figure. Even for toddlers growing up in a highly R/S household or culture, that capacity may not emerge until between age 2 and 3 (or beyond), once their capacity for *mentalizing* (the ability to understand, interpret, and respond to the intentional, self-directed mental states of oneself and others; White, 2021) emerges and begins maturing.

Psychoanalysts Winnicott (1975/1992) and Rizzuto (1979) have explained how this process often unfolds. Winnicott (1975/1992) suggested that, around age 4 to 6 months, infants develop the psychological capacity to rely on concrete "transitional objects" (p. 229; a pacifier, familiar blanket, or favorite stuffed animal) for comfort and support, especially when they are separated physically from their caregiver(s). Winnicott (1975/1992) and Rizzuto (1979) posited that over time, as the infant–toddler develops a greater capacity for symbolic thought (the ability to hold a mental representation of a person or object in mind) by around age 18 to 24 months, the mental representation of a "living God" (Rizzuto, 1979, p. 41) might also be birthed. This anthropomorphized God representation may start serving as a transitional object, eventually becoming a core foundation for the child's R/S development.

3.2.2 Early Childhood (Preschool-Aged Children)

Many core acquisitions underlying R/S development unfold during early childhood (~ages 3–6). Even in the first year of life, infants and toddlers begin to develop malleable mental/neural representations of themselves, others (e.g., primary caregivers), and the world. They may develop a nascent mental/neural representation of God towards the end of toddlerhood. Across early childhood, the child's mental/neural representations of themselves, others, and the world (*internal working models*) grow considerably in complexity and in how much they are based in symbolic thought (vs. in sensorimotor input during infancy–toddlerhood). This occurs as the child's relationships with their primary attachment figure(s) continue(s) to evolve, deepening in emotional and cognitive complexity while broadening in contextual applicability and flexibility. These developments are a function of (a) repeated interaction sequences that corroborate/refine the child's attachment representations and (b) the child's maturing language and cognitive abilities (Granqvist, 2020). Two particularly key cognitive developments emerge in latter toddlerhood and early childhood:

- *mentalization* (the ability to understand, interpret, and predict the responses of self and others in terms underlying mental states such as thoughts, feelings, intentions, desires, and perceptions; Fonagy et al., 2002) and
- *theory of mind* (the ability to attribute mental states to oneself and others while also understanding that others' mental states can differ from one's own and can be false; Wellman et al., 2001).

Children who have experienced recurrent security-enhancing interactions with their caregiver(s) can now understand that caregiver separation (and other formerly distressing attachment threats) do not necessitate overt attachment behaviors like crying or following. This is because the child has developed internalized mental representations of (a) their caregiver(s) as planning to come back and as caring for and protecting them even while away and (b) themselves as loved and capable of caring for themselves while physically separated from their caregiver(s). These types of mental representations are called *security-based self-representations* because they are derived from internalized security-enhancing interactions with attachment figures (see Section 7 and Figure 5). Gradually, these security-based self-representations help reduce the child's reliance on the attachment figure's physical availability during times of stress/distress (Bowlby, 1973; Mikulincer & Shaver, 2004).

With the emergence of mentalization and theory of mind, the child can also have mind-related conversations with caregiver(s) and others. Whenever these conversations are not deceptive, they offer opportunities to expand the child's understanding of themselves and others and to facilitate relational repair when needed. To illustrate, if a child is at a store with their caregiver and the caregiver unintentionally gets separated, when the caregiver realizes it and finds the frightened child, the caregiver can hug the child and say: "I am so sorry! I did not *mean* to walk away from you! I *thought* you saw where I was and were following me. Please forgive me." Accompanied by compassionate hugs, these types of mentalizing comments (*italicized*) can restore the child's confidence they are loved and their caregiver is accessible and has benevolent intentions. The child can begin realizing their caregiver's mind is truly what drives their caregiver's behavior. Even if the caregiver's behaviors are occasionally imperfect, the child can mentally represent the "good-enough" caregiver's mind as available, responsive, and loving (Granqvist, 2020; Winnicott, 1975/1992).

Because these types of mentalizing interactions afford increased flexibility and collaboration in the child–caregiver relationship, Bowlby (1969/1982) called this last phase of attachment-relationship development the "goal-corrected partnership" (p. 267). The child now can have insights into the caregiver's mental states (feelings, thoughts, intentions, etc.), and the child and caregiver can influence each other to adjust behaviors to achieve shared goals (e.g., safety, security, repair, or autonomy-supportiveness within developmentally appropriate parameters). During early childhood, the child's attachment functioning becomes governed more by experienced-gained, symbolic insights than by the trial-and-error, sensorimotor reactivity of infancy–toddlerhood (Bowlby, 1969/1982).

Naturally, these cognitive and attachment-related developments have vast implications for R/S development. Even young children raised in nonreligious homes often develop mental representations of God(s) and other supernatural beings. Some scholars argue this phenomenon is because children universally are prepared cognitively to represent some minds as having supernatural knowledge and abilities. Other scholars argue it is because children universally tend to *anthropomorphize* (attribute human-like characteristics and abilities to non-human objects or beings; White, 2021). Regardless, not only do young children normatively develop god representations, but in attachment-activating situations, they also may normatively represent God(s) as a safe haven. This finding has been replicated with children in Italy (Cassibba et al., 2013) and Sweden (Granqvist et al., 2007b).

However, children raised in R/S homes and cultures are probably more apt to develop an actual *attachment relationship* with God(s). This may be especially likely for children raised in a home, place, or tradition where God is prototypically viewed more as a person than an impersonal force. That would include children raised in Abrahamic-faith homes, cultures, or traditions (Christianity,

Judaism, or Islam), which are more prevalent in Africa, North and South America, Australia–Oceania, and the Middle East (relative to East and South Asia, where other religions are usually more prevalent; Pew Research Center, 2012).

In sum, our discussion of early childhood illustrates the pivotal role of social–cultural learning in co-sculpting (amplifying or weakening) the expression of attachment maturation on children's R/S development (see Section 5 more on social–cultural learning). The influence of social–cultural learning continues growing as children transition from early to middle childhood. During early childhood, social–cultural learning primarily may affect the child's developing *spirituality*, whereas during middle childhood, it may more strongly shape their developing *religiousness* (Granqvist, 2020).

3.2.3 Middle Childhood (School-Aged Children)

During middle childhood (~age 6–12), the child's attachment representations and dispositions continue to evolve in complexity. School-aged children refine their attachment representations through the greater depth and breadth of relational interactions they have with primary caregivers and surrogate attachment figures. Because their cognitive capacities for mentalization and symbolization are maturing rapidly, children can begin understanding and predicting others' behavior. If their attachment figures have provided consistent availability and sensitivity, the child's developing sense of self-worth, self-esteem, and self-confidence are typically positive and increasingly stable. Likewise, their views, perceptions, and expectations of others are generally positive. These mental/neural representations of self and others become increasingly consolidated and generalizable (Cassidy & Shaver, 2016; cf. Vannucci et al., 2025).

As began in early childhood, children in middle childhood rely increasingly on internalized attachment representations rather than actual physical proximity to attachment figures. Additionally, rather than relying on attachment figures to help coregulate their emotions and downregulate their attachment-related distress, school-aged children gradually learn to regulate their own emotions, stress, and distress, partly by relying on internalized security-based representations of self, others, and relationships (self-with-others). They also are developing better psychological capacities for empathizing, perspective-taking, self-regulating, and coping. They are building better social skills like learning how to make/keep friends and resolve conflicts. They may be developing competencies in academics, sports, or other hobbies, affording a greater sense of self-efficacy, mastery, and goal-orientation. They are learning to face challenging tasks and persist in accomplishing them. In sum, normative attachment development in middle childhood involves substantial growth in internalized attachment security, which thereby leads to many positive outcomes (Cassidy & Shaver, 2016; Mikulincer & Shaver, 2016, 2023a, 2023b).

As school-aged children grow in internalized security, they broaden their focus to the extrafamilial world of school, peers, and leisure activities. They start preferring to spend time with their peers, not their parents (Cassidy & Shaver, 2016). Peer friendships marked by trust and companionship become hugely important for their well-being and ongoing development (Hartup, 1996). Because school-aged children's attachment system is activated less readily (due to internalized security), matters of attachment may seem to play a smaller role in children's everyday lives (Bowlby, 1969/1982). Yet by no means does attachment become obsolete or irrelevant. For instance, school-aged children who have difficulty forming friendships and receive little emotional support and engagement from caregiver(s) will often experience painful loneliness due to the perceived absence of meaningful attachment bonds (Granqvist, 2020; Weiss, 1973).

Regarding R/S development and attachment, school-aged children develop more advanced meaning-making capacities, and those capacities can lead them to rely more heavily on religious narratives (Fowler, 1987) in their developing R/S attachment relationship. Moreover, even as they are beginning to develop their own *narrative identity* (the internalized "stories people have in their minds about how they have come to be the particular people they are becoming," McAdams, 2021, p. 123), they may also begin developing their own *transcendent narrative identity* (their internalized, evolving story about themselves and how they fit into a story bigger than themselves; Schnitker et al., 2019). Their transcendent narrative identity can often center on their attachment relationship with God(s).

Research on preschool- and school-aged children has revealed several insights. Preschool-aged children tend to view and relate with God(s) in quite human-like (parent-like) ways, whereas school-aged children often view and relate with God(s) as more superhuman (divine-like, supernatural; de Roos et al., 2003). Nonetheless, school-aged children report experiencing God as emotionally and personally closer (i.e., more of an attachment figure) than preschool-aged children do (Eshleman et al., 1999; Tamminen, 1994). In fact, even in Finland (a highly secularized nation), Tamminen (1994) found that 40% of school-aged children reported feeling especially close to God during situations of loneliness or perceived danger.

Importantly, for children raised in R/S homes and cultures, their religiousness/spirituality and R/S attachment become increasingly systematized (schematized) during middle childhood. A school-aged R/S child usually develops a faith and relationship with God(s) based strongly on their culturally or familially available religious texts and systems of beliefs, morals, values, stories, and rituals. Comparatively, school-aged children raised in non-R/S homes or cultures may begin leaving behind noncorporeal attachment figures, viewing them as no longer believable or psychologically needed (Granqvist, 2020).

3.2.4 Adolescence and Young Adulthood

Adolescence (~ages 12–18) and young adulthood (~ages 18–30) involve rapid physical, cognitive, emotional, and social development. Partly because profound brain development occurs during this period (Cozolino, 2024; Lerner & Steinberg, 2009), the attachment maturation and development that unfolds during one's teenage and young adult years has a tremendous impact on the trajectories of one's adult life (Cassidy & Shaver, 2016).

Psychologically, there are two major developmental tasks of adolescence – identity development (Erikson, 1959/1994) and developing a culturally normative degree of autonomy from primary caregivers (Granqvist, 2020). Attachment plays a key role in each. Adolescents acquire increasing cognitive abilities to think abstractly, reason hypothetically, make planful decisions, engage in complex socioemotional/moral reasoning, and navigate complex personal/interpersonal situations. Their growing striving toward achieving parental autonomy (Lerner & Steinberg, 2009) usually coincides with their growing (and sometimes inappropriate/unwise) dependence on friends and romantic partners. As the adolescent aspires toward autonomy, attachment functions steadily transfer from parents to peers. Peers help support the adolescent's autonomy and identity development (Granqvist, 2020; Siegel, 2020).

Adolescents' attachment formation with peers unfolds analogously to how it unfolded with their early caregivers (Cassidy & Shaver, 2016). The proximity-seeking attachment function is transferred from parents to peers during middle childhood, then it climaxes in adolescence as the safe-haven function is transferred, and eventually it culminates in young adulthood as the secure-base function is transferred. Research across the world – in Australia (Feeney, 2004), China (Zhang et al., 2011), the United States (Fraley & Davis, 1997), and Germany and Sweden (Friedlmeier & Granqvist, 2006) – has now supported this stepwise attachment-transferring process. There may be minor cultural differences regarding timing (e.g., the secure-base function may get transferred a bit later in many collectivistic societies), and the transferring of the secure-base function is likely affected by pertinent contextual factors (e.g., romantic relationship status in young adulthood; Granqvist, 2020). Typically, long-term romantic partners are selected as the principal attachment figures of adulthood (Bowlby, 1980), and attachment is the emotional "glue" that binds romantic partners together (Granqvist, 2020; Mikulincer & Shaver, 2016).

Yet, despite how straightforward this transferring process might seem, it can be a long, difficult, and winding road. Many young adults hit several romantic-relationship dead ends before at last seeming to find "the One," only to end up in a heartbreaking separation and starting all over. When considering such winding roads, attachment-related individual differences often play a role (see Section 4; Granqvist, 2020).

There are a few more key issues for understanding adolescent and young adult R/S development vis-à-vis attachment. Even as adolescence and young adulthood are periods of profound attachment maturation and development, they can also be characterized by profound changes in religiousness/spirituality. Many adolescents and young adults become more R/S during this phase (Hood et al., 2018; Smith & Denton, 2009; Smith & Snell, 2009). Many others who were raised R/S become less R/S during it (Pew Research Center, 2018, 2020). They might even *religiously deconstruct* (break down and struggle with their religion/spirituality), *reconstruct* (expand or rebuild their religion/spirituality in self-determined ways), and/or *deidentify* (leave religion/spirituality altogether; Van Tongeren, 2024).

Over a century ago, William James (1902) observed that aspects of religion/spirituality appealed particularly to adolescent sentiments. As we have seen, the cognitive machinery for R/S belief and practice has typically been in place since early childhood, but adolescence is often when the emotional fuel gushes into that machinery (Granqvist, 2020). Adolescence and young adulthood are also the life phases that are most distinctly associated with sudden religious conversions and other spiritually transformative experiences (Hood et al., 2018). There are several reasons for the increased religiousness/spirituality that many adolescents and young adults experience. We, of course, do not deny that numerous processes and influences are involved, but the attachment transferring process is one plausible explanation (Granqvist, 2020). Relinquishing one's parents as the primary source of attachment-need fulfillment can leave an emotional vacuum (Weiss, 1973). Emotionally satisfying and stable relationships with peers can be difficult to come by and even more difficult to maintain, possibly leaving adolescents with a painful socioemotional void that has few, if any, need-satisfying attachments. In this situation, they might turn to God as a surrogate attachment figure (Granqvist, 2020). Even for adolescents and young adults who successfully develop strong attachment relationships with friends and romantic partners, they might perceive God as serving attachment functions in ways even their best friend or partner cannot (e.g., helping provide spiritual or moral clarity on difficult, consequential decisions).

Likewise, for adolescents and young adults who choose to become less R/S or to religiously/spiritually reconstruct, many shift from practicing a traditional religion toward practicing a more private, individualized spirituality. That spirituality may center on their perceived attachment relationship with God(s) or other divine/divine-like figures (the Universe, Ultimate Truth, True Self, etc.). Still others may stay irreligious/nonspiritual or become more so over time (Van Tongeren, 2024).

Again, a critical question here is, why do some adolescents and young adults become increasingly attached to God whereas others do not? Answers to that question often relate to the contextual factors and attachment-related individual differences discussed in Part III.

3.2.5 Middle and Older Adulthood

As with adult development generally (Nelson & Dannifer, 1992), attachment development becomes exceedingly diverse, suggesting individual and cultural differences make it hard to characterize "normative" adult attachment development (Granqvist, 2020; Mikulincer & Shaver, 2016). Even so, as Freud (1953–1974), Erikson (1959/1980), and Kübler-Ross (1969) have posited, four major psychological tasks characterize cross-culturally normative adult development – love, work, generativity, and death. There is widespread public consensus that navigating each task well is central to psychologically healthy adult development, and attachment experts generally concur (Cassidy & Shaver, 2016; Mikulincer & Shaver, 2016).

For most adults, the domain of love not only includes romantic pair-bonds but also love for one's children. Caring for one's children is a major way that adults channel their strivings for generativity. But loving one's romantic partner is typically what adults find the most challenging (while hopefully still rewarding). Adults' challenges in navigating romantic attachment relationships are unsurprising considering that a healthy long-term romantic attachment requires successfully nurturing and maintaining the integration of several behavioral systems (attachment, sex, caregiving, etc.) and doing so within oneself, with one's partner, and within the dyad (Bowlby, 1980; Mikulincer & Shaver, 2016). Perhaps because that is so hard – especially given attachment-related individual differences (Section 4) – divorce and recurrent break-ups are on the verge of becoming normative. A large and increasing percentage of adults are choosing to stay unpartnered, or they have trouble finding and maintaining a long-term partnership. Nonetheless, unpartnered adults tend to report poorer health and economic outcomes, relative to partnered adults (Granqvist, 2020; Pew Research Center, 2021).

Regarding love for one's children, adults' parent–child bonds are often among the most rewarding relationships in their lives. Those long-but-short years of parenting are frequently characterized by love and joy, but they also can come with ample stress, frustration, worry, and sleep deprivation. The constant balancing act of caregiving, romantic-partner, and work investments mean that many middle-aged adults are overly busy, stretched, and exhausted. Thankfully, bonding keeps most caregivers committed to their children, fueled by an abiding sense of fulfilling and generative love (Cassidy & Shaver, 2016; Granqvist, 2020).

Regarding R/S development during middle adulthood, this developmental phase is frequently marked by R/S stability (conservation of current R/S beliefs and practices, including a perceived relationship with God, if applicable) and intergenerational transmission of caregiver (non)religion/(non)spirituality to children. That is, barring some life-transformative event (e.g., falling in love with a partner whose religion/spirituality differs significantly from oneself; experiencing profound trauma, struggle, or loss; or developing a terminal or chronic illness), middle adulthood is usually *not* a period of substantial R/S change. Instead, it is when an adult's habits are nurtured and passed down to their children, if they have any. Interestingly, growing evidence suggests religion/spirituality (and a collectively shared relationship with God) helps many families form and maintain strong relational/attachment bonds and might help some families experience positive transformative growth. This possibility, of course, depends heavily on familial contextual factors and on individual differences in human attachment and religion/spirituality (Hood et al., 2018; Mahoney, 2010).

As Section 3 concludes, we discuss life's final phase – older adulthood. Older adults face similar personal, interpersonal, financial, and occupational stressors as their younger counterparts. Yet additionally, older adults face unique challenges, such as an uncertain transition out of the workforce, the recurrent losses of loved ones (siblings, friends, a long-term partner), and the common decline of physical (and/or cognitive) health and social support. The grief and mourning that accompanies these losses can be immense and destabilizing, especially the death of a spouse (Bowlby, 1980; Mikulincer & Shaver, 2016).

But many older adults continue to flourish amidst such challenges. Erikson (1959/1980) described such elderly people as having achieved wisdom and a sense of psychological integrity (a feeling their life's meaning makes coherent and redemptive sense, their life has been well-lived, and they can face death with calmness, acceptance, and generativity). Attachment relationships with family members and close friends can help nurture this healthy state of mind.

Another health-facilitating developmental process that often emerges in older adulthood is *gerotranscendence* (Tornstam, 2011) – a positive aging process by which older people demonstrate "a shift in meta-perspective, from a materialistic and rational view of the world to a more cosmic and transcendent one, normally accompanied by an increase in life satisfaction" (Tornstam, 2011, p. 166). Frequently, older adults' R/S attachment to God plays a key role in this positive developmental process (Abreu et al., 2023). Many older people experience a broader R/S "awakening," especially during times of great attachment loss such as spousal bereavement or terminal illness (Brown et al., 2004).

3.3 Conclusion

In Section 3, we argued that R/S development arises from general developmental maturation, which itself stems from interactions between specific genetic dispositions and recurrent exposure to certain environmental input (from relationships, culture, etc.). We described the infancy and toddlerhood period (~age 0–3 years) as a pre-R/S phase that nonetheless has unparalleled impact on what eventually emerges as R/S development. The attachment functions that caregivers serve may start being filled by a mentally "living" God representation. During early childhood (~age 3–6), young children often have religiously/spiritually colored ideas and experiences, regardless of whether they are raised in an R/S family or society. However, middle childhood (~age 6–12) is usually a time of major socializing influence from the child's surrounding social figures – caregivers, peers, teachers, and so forth. The nascent spirituality of early childhood gradually conforms more closely to the socially and culturally defined R/S (or non-R/S) norms in their social ecosystem (Granqvist, 2020).

Adolescence and young adulthood are times of transition and exploration, as young people question and define their R/S identity, including whether an attachment relationship with God is something they want to continue, discontinue, or begin. Often such decisions are influenced heavily by peers and romantic partners. Similarly, middle age is commonly a time of R/S conservation/stability, as adults continue practicing whatever (non)religion/(non)spirituality they have and pass that down to any children they may have had. As they navigate the final phase of life, older adults might find themselves spiritually (re)vitalized through a common, positive developmental process of gerotranscendence (Granqvist, 2020; Tornstam, 2011) that can help them navigate common challenges of older adulthood.

Part III Individual Differences in Forms and Processes of Attachment and Religion/Spirituality

Part III transitions from the foundational commonalities discussed in Part II to the important particulars of human attachment and religion/spirituality. Section 4 summarizes theory and research on individual differences in human attachment. The next two Sections describe the main ways that individual differences in human attachment and religion/spirituality develop and manifest – the "correspondence" facet (Section 5) and "compensation" facet (Section 6). In each case, the term *facet* can refer both to the initial development of individual differences in R/S attachment (stemming from developed individual differences in human attachment) and to subsequent manifestations of corresponding or compensatory individual differences in human attachment and religion/spirituality.

4 Individual Differences in Human Attachment

"Each of us is apt to do unto others as we have been done by."
— John Bowlby (1979/2005, p. 166)

So far, we have focused on how humans *normatively* approach attachment relationships with people and God(s). Next, we discuss how and why people *differ* in their attachment representations, dispositions, and habits. Section 4 has four parts. First, we describe attachment-related individual differences at the conceptual level. Second, we review the scientific literature on continuity and variation in these individual differences across relationships and time. Third, we highlight several determinants of attachment-related individual differences. Last, we provide a sobering reminder that the study and practical applications of attachment theory are much broader than individual differences.

4.1 Conceptual Considerations

Just as all people have a unique profile of personality characteristics that differentiate them, everyone has a distinguishing profile of attachment representations, dispositions, and habits. Similarly, just as one's personality is formed and transformed through a lifetime of interactions between nature (genes) and nurture (environmental input, particularly from relationships and culture; John & Robins, 2021), everyone's attachment representations and dispositions/habits are formed and transformed through a lifetime of gene–environment interaction, also mainly via relationships and culture (Dugan et al., 2025). Psychologists define *individual differences* as identifiable variations in how people think, feel, behave, and/or relate. These differences are the distinguishable ways people vary in their cognitive, emotional, behavioral, and relational patterns and attributes (Chamorro-Premuzic et al., 2015).

Contemporary attachment scholars usually consider four major forms (types) of attachment-related individual differences: *secure, insecure–avoidant/dismissing, insecure–resistant/preoccupied,* and *disorganized–disoriented/unresolved* (Ainsworth et al., 1978; Main & Solomon, 1990). Those unpersuaded that typologies are the best way to describe individual differences in attachment often emphasize the underlying continuous dimensions of *attachment avoidance* and *anxiety* (Brennan et al., 1998).

We adopt a *both/and* approach to understanding attachment-related individual differences. Both the categorical-prototype and the continuous-dimensional conceptualizations have strengths and limitations, and each approach is pragmatically useful under certain conditions. We appreciate recent efforts to integrate these approaches into a unified framework (Raby et al., 2021). Although we later describe Raby and colleagues' (2021) integrated conceptual framework (see Section 4.4), we first will summarize theory and research that has adopted *either* a categorical-prototype approach *or* a continuous-dimensional approach. The reason for that is because attachment experts have fiercely debated which approach is more valid and useful, to the point that experts from each "camp" have conducted their work mostly in parallel, resulting in a rather nonintegrated and ironically nonattuned field of attachment science (Granqvist, 2020).

4.2 Individual Differences from a Categorical-Prototype Framework

The categorical-prototype framework conceptualizes attachment-related individual differences into three organized patterns of attachment – *secure, insecure–avoidant/dismissing,* and *insecure–resistant/preoccupied* (Ainsworth et al., 1978) – along with a fourth form called *disorganized–disoriented/unresolved* attachment (Main & Solomon, 1990). Each form of attachment has parallel forms in infancy/early childhood and adolescence/adulthood. Importantly, during infancy and early childhood, attachment dispositions/habits are mainly classified based on attachment-relevant *behaviors*. During adolescence and adulthood, they are mainly classified based on *representational products* (e.g., language/speech, drawings, or behaviorally observable enactments; Granqvist, 2020).

4.2.1 Secure Attachment Disposition

Prevalence Rates

Globally, an estimated 52% of infants (Madigan et al., 2023) and 50% of adolescents and adults exhibit a principal secure attachment disposition (Bakermans-Kranenburg et al., 2024). There may be minor variations based on geographical, personal, or sociocultural factors. However, meta-analyses have found stark differences in prevalence rates when comparing nonclinical samples (people from the general population) either with clinical samples (when the infant/caregiver or adolescent/adult has one or more mental disorder) or with other at-risk samples (when the infant/caregiver or adolescent/adult has one or more personal or sociocultural risk factor present, such as low socioeconomic status, lifetime trauma/abuse exposure, adopted/fostered status, or a medical/mental/neurodevelopmental condition). For instance, among infants, the estimated rate of a principal secure attachment is only 14% among infants who have experienced caregiver maltreatment, relative to those who have not (53%), and it is only 42% among infants raised in a low socioeconomic status environment (vs. not: 55%; Madigan et al., 2023). Among adults, the estimated rate of principal secure attachment is 50% in nonclinical, non-risk samples but only 23% in clinical and 36% in at-risk samples (Bakermans-Kranenburg et al., 2024).

Defining Features

One way to characterize the defining features of a secure attachment disposition is to recall the defining features of a normative attachment bond. A person with a secure attachment disposition exhibits a solid fit to these normative features. They

- seek and maintain proximity to their actual or internalized attachment figure(s) when distressed (*proximity seeking/maintenance function*),
- display attachment behaviors toward their attachment figure(s) when their attachment system is mentally/neurally activated (*safe-haven function*),
- rely psychologically on these security-enhancing figures/representations for both hope and confidence whenever this system is nonactivated (*secure-base function*), and
- respond to actual/perceived separation with distress and to actual/perceived loss with grief (but become psychologically reorganized in due course).

Although individuals with an insecure or disorganized attachment exhibit some degree of fit to these normative features, they also exhibit inconsistency or psychological defensiveness of various kinds (Ainsworth, 1989; Bowlby, 1969/1982; Granqvist, 2020).

Research has revealed other defining features of a secure attachment disposition. For instance, hundreds of studies have found support for Main's (1990) parsimonious account of what fundamentally distinguishes secure vs. insecure/disorganized attachment across the lifespan. Main (1990) claimed that secure attachment is characterized by *flexibility of attention to attachment-related information*, whereas insecure and disorganized attachments are characterized by a rigidity (insecure) or breakdown (disorganized) of attention to attachment-related information. For individuals with a principal secure attachment, when their attachment system gets activated mentally/neurally (e.g., they are distressed or separated from their attachment figure), their attention reliably and often rapidly turns to attachment (e.g., infants: visually locating their caregiver[s]; adolescents/adults: contacting their attachment figure[s] by phone or text). Securely attached individuals tend to be easily soothed by their actual or internalized attachment figures. Hence, when their attachment system is deactivated (e.g., infants: by reunion with their caregiver[s]; adolescents/adults: by restoration of felt security via security-enhancing interaction with their attachment figure[s] or by activation of security-based self-representations), their attention switches to other concerns like exploring their environment or re-engaging in daily concerns (Granqvist, 2020; Mikulincer & Shaver, 2016).

More broadly, secure attachment is marked by a high degree of *integration* ("the linkage of differentiated elements," Siegel, 2020, p. 461), both structurally and functionally. There is coherence both at the level of

- their mental/neural representations (*structural integration*; e.g., they have positively valenced and nondefensive attachment representations of themselves, others, and the world) and
- the explicit (more-conscious) and implicit (less-conscious) layers of their mental/neural responses and information processing (*functional integration*).

Their social behavioral systems reliably work together in an adaptive, well-coordinated manner (Ainsworth et al., 1978; Bowlby, 1973; Granqvist, 2020).

Because of this high level of integration, youth and adults who have a principal secure attachment disposition usually communicate in a coherent (easily comprehendible and interpretable), open (collaborative and receptive), fluid (free-flowing), credible (detailed and evidence-substantiated), and psychologically nondefensive (authentic and self-aware) way (Main et al., 2003; Siegel, 2020). They readily communicate their own needs, thoughts, desires, and emotions, and they respond sensitively to those of others. They have a generally realistic and accurate perception of themselves, others, and situations (Granqvist, 2020). Their memories of relational experiences are reality-based and can be substantiated by consciously accessible and credibly articulated *episodic memories* ("conscious knowledge of temporally dated, spatially located, and personally experienced events or episodes," Smith & Kosslyn, 2007, p. 194). Furthermore, when securely attached people describe socioemotionally significant memories, they do so in an emotionally well-regulated manner, using free and autonomous communication that is not overwhelmed by psychophysiological distress or dysregulation (Granqvist, 2020; Main et al., 2003).

Youth and adults with a principal secure attachment disposition value their attachment relationships but exhibit appropriate autonomy from them. They invest in and cultivate these relationships. They lean into resolving interpersonal conflicts that arise. They can fully forgive and be fully forgiven. They seek and nurture closeness/intimacy, mutuality/reciprocity, and culturally normative interdependence (depending on each other for emotional and practical support; Granqvist, 2020; Mikulincer & Shaver, 2016, 2023a, 2023b).

Initially, a secure attachment develops as a natural function of receiving sensitive caregiving, which consolidates the evolved human-inborn expectation of sensitive care (as evident in crying and other signaling behaviors). For this reason, secure attachment is often understood as the primary (evolutionarily preprogrammed) attachment strategy (Main, 1990).

Importantly, some adolescents or adults who have had significant negative experiences with their childhood caregivers are eventually able to discuss those experiences in a coherent, relationally collaborative, and emotionally well-regulated way. These individuals are typically classified as having an experientially "earned" secure attachment. Such a disposition commonly reflects the person's sincere efforts to understand their caregiver(s) compassionately, acknowledge their caregivers' shortcomings (while placing them in a broader social and intergenerational context), and adopt empathic and forgiving attitudes toward their caregivers (Cassidy & Shaver, 2016; Granqvist, 2020).

4.2.2 Insecure–Avoidant/Dismissing Attachment Disposition

Prevalence Rates

Globally, the estimated prevalence of a principal insecure–avoidant/dismissing attachment disposition is around 15% in infants (Madigan et al., 2023), 33% in adolescents, and 25% in adults (Bakermans-Kranenburg et al., 2024). An insecure–avoidant disposition is slightly more prevalent among infants raised in a low socioeconomic-status context (18% vs. not: 14%; Madigan et al., 2023). Among adults, there are no major differences in the estimated prevalence rate among nonclinical, non-risk adults (25%), relative to clinical (26%) or at-risk (27%) adults (Bakermans-Kranenburg et al., 2024).

Defining Features

One defining feature of an insecure–avoidant/dismissing attachment disposition is that the person exhibits *attentional rigidity by actively avoiding thinking about or feeling attachment-related concerns*. They have an attachment-minimizing attentional focus and hence might be described as *attachment underactivated and underreliant*. They usually do not protest when separated from attachment figure(s); instead, they may appear indifferent. Even when their attachment system is activated, they may rigidly and defensively maintain attentional focus on nonattachment matters. They might neither seek proximity to their attachment figure(s) nor rely much on them as a safe haven or secure base. Instead, they defensively rely on themselves to navigate life and stressful situations. They frequently engage in defensive self-reliance and self-enhancement, convincing themselves and others they do not need anyone. They often avoid intimacy, closeness, and (inter)dependence as much as reasonably possible (Granqvist, 2020; Mikulincer & Shaver, 2016).

Individuals with a principal insecure–avoidant/dismissing attachment disposition usually place an implicitly low value on attachment and relationships. However, this low value may not be readily apparent, because their mental/neural representations of themselves and others are often poorly integrated (incoherent). At the implicit (less-conscious) level, these individuals typically have negative mental/neural representations of others, viewing others as intrusive, rejecting, unavailable, or controlling. Yet at the explicit (consciously articulatable) level, they frequently describe having positive, idealistic views of others (e.g., "My dad was extremely loving" or "My spouse is perfect"), without being able to substantiate those claims with detailed, credible episodic memories (Granqvist, 2020; Main et al., 2003).

These individuals often have self-representations that are equally incoherent. They commonly hold implicit negative beliefs and feelings about themselves, avoiding attachment figures because they nonconsciously feel unworthy of love, care, or esteem. However, the explicit self-representations they describe to others (and self-deceptively believe about themselves) are defensively positive, conveying a strong, self-reliant, capable person who does not need anyone. Taken together, individuals with a principal insecure–avoidant/dismissing attachment disposition have poorly integrated and often contradictory mental/neural representations of themselves and others.

Moreover, adolescents/adults with a principal insecure–dismissing attachment disposition usually communicate in a closed, defensive, and vague way when it comes to talking about their thoughts, feelings, needs, and desires (Siegel, 2020). They have a hard time self-disclosing anything socioemotionally meaningful, particularly if it could be perceived as negative or weak about themselves. Instead, they tend to communicate about more surface-level or abstract (vague, overintellectualized) topics, because those topics keep emotions and relational partners at a "safe" emotional distance. They frequently have difficulty with insightful awareness (of themselves and others) and may not perceive or recall situations realistically or straightforwardly (due to defensive self-enhancement; Granqvist, 2020; Mikulincer & Shaver, 2016).

Regarding the determinants of an insecure–avoidant/dismissing attachment disposition, oftentimes this disposition develops as a function of the person receiving relatively insensitive (distant, rejecting, or intrusive) caregiving.

Because their proximity-seeking and other attachment-signaling behaviors (e.g., of the need for a safe haven and secure base) were often unsuccessful, they learned to suppress the activation of their attachment system. They developed an emotion-minimizing and defensively self-reliant strategy for coping with distress and relational separation (Granqvist, 2020; Mikulincer & Shaver, 2016). This avoidance presumably developed as a secondary (experience-evolved) attachment strategy, because the evolutionarily inborn primary (secure proximity-seeking) attachment strategy failed (Main, 1990).

4.2.3 Insecure–Resistant/Preoccupied Attachment Disposition

Prevalence Rates

The estimated global prevalence of a principal insecure–resistant/preoccupied attachment disposition is 10% in infants (Madigan et al., 2023), 6% in adolescents, and 8% in adults. Among adults, rates of this attachment disposition are similar when nonclinical, non-risk adults (8%) are compared to clinical (12%) and at-risk (8%) adults (Bakermans-Kranenburg et al., 2024).

Defining Features

People with an insecure–resistant/preoccupied attachment disposition typically exhibit *attentional rigidity through an overfocus on attachment-related concerns*. They have an attachment-maximizing (negative) attentional focus and hence can be described as *attachment overactivated and overreliant*. Their attachment system is activated easily and quickly, and when it is, they react with marked passivity, anger, or both. They experience and express intense emotional reactions to perceived separation (helplessness, despair, etc.), often misinterpreting the separation as a sign of rejection or insufficient love/care. When their attachment figure "finally" offers help, the attached person may angrily rebuff/resist their attempts. People with an insecure–resistant/preoccupied attachment disposition struggle to calm down and shift their attention to nonattachment matters like exploration. They also often struggle to take developmentally appropriate agentic initiative and responsibility (Granqvist, 2020).

Individuals with a principal insecure–resistant/preoccupied attachment disposition typically have negative implicit and explicit mental/neural representations of themselves. They view themselves as unlovable, incapable (passive/helpless), and unworthy of love/care. Nevertheless, their intense anger and protest over separation can signal an underlying feeling they are worthy of more care than they are currently getting. Hence, their mental/neural representations of others are also incoherent. Others are viewed paradoxically both as capable rescuers who can soothe/save them and as unreliable, disappointing, and untrustworthy sources of care (Granqvist, 2020).

People with a principal insecure–resistant/preoccupied attachment disposition often communicate their feelings, needs, and desires in a dramatic or demanding way. This communication strategy is especially likely if they think their attachment figure is paying more attention to someone or something besides them. If so, they might respond with intense jealousy or even rage, becoming preoccupied with regaining their attachment figure's attention and care. Unfortunately, their emotionally dysregulated communication is often experienced as manipulative, irritating, or cumbersome. Attachment figures might grow weary of trying to support and please them, because these individuals frequently claim to value attachment/intimacy but their negative attentional bias makes them prone to overfocusing on their attachment figures' shortcomings (Granqvist, 2020).

4.2.4 Disorganized–Disoriented/Unresolved Attachment

Prevalence Rates

The estimated global prevalence rate of a principal disorganized–disoriented/unresolved attachment is 24% in infants (Madigan et al., 2023), 11% in adolescents, and 17% in adults (Bakermans-Kranenburg et al., 2024), but once more, these rates can vary. Infants raised in a low socioeconomic status context might exhibit higher rates of disorganized–disoriented attachment (31% vs. not: 21%). Other groups of infants who are at increased likelihood of disorganized–disoriented attachment include: infants who are fostered/adopted (40% vs. not: 23%), infants who have experienced caregiver maltreatment (abuse or neglect; 65% vs. not: 22%), and infants whose caregiver experienced maltreatment during their own childhood (39% vs. not: 23%; Madigan et al., 2023).

Among adults, principal disorganized–unresolved attachment is much more prevalent in at-risk (31%) and clinical adult samples (40%) than in nonclinical, non-risk adult samples (17%). It also is highly prevalent among adults who experienced childhood maltreatment (40%; Bakermans-Kranenburg et al., 2024).

Defining Features

The insecure patterns of attachment (avoidant/dismissing and resistant/preoccupied) are understood as *organized* (secondary) strategies for responding to suboptimal caregiving. In contrast, disorganized–disoriented/unresolved attachment is understood as reflecting an experience-based habitual breakdown (*dis*organization) in attention and behavior that occurs when the person feels highly threatened or distressed (Main & Solomon, 1990). Disorganized–

disoriented/unresolved attachment can take on many forms. For instance, Main and Solomon (1990) identified several indicators of a principal disorganized–disoriented attachment in infants who were present with their caregivers during the Strange Situation assessment procedure. Infants who displayed a good fit to one or more indicators were classified as exhibiting a principal disorganized–disoriented attachment:

- sequential and simultaneous displays of contradictory behavioral responses;
- nondirected, misdirected, interrupted, or incomplete movements/expressions;
- movements or postures that were highly unusual (repetitive, mistimed, asymmetrical, etc.);
- frozen, stilled, or slowed movements/expressions;
- marked indications of apprehension toward the caregiver; or
- other clear indications of disorganization or disorientation.

What leads to a principal disorganized–disoriented attachment classification is the intensity and timing of the infant's disorganized/disoriented behavior. Consequently, infants (and adolescents/adults) who exhibit this principal classification are also given a secondary "best-fitting" classification for the organized attachment strategy they most prototypically employ (e.g., disorganized/avoidant-dismissing or disorganized/resistant-preoccupied attachment; Granqvist, 2020).

In adolescence and adulthood, disorganized–unresolved attachment is often characterized by noticeable lapses in reasoning or communicational coherence in response to loss (through death) and/or relational trauma (abuse or neglect). These lapses are specifically evident when the person discusses the unresolved event(s) or is exposed to situations that somehow remind them traumatically of the event(s) (Granqvist, 2020).

When it comes to their mental/neural representations, people with a principal disorganized–disoriented/unresolved attachment usually have highly disintegrated (incoherent) representations of themselves and others. These representations get mentally/neurally activated frequently, especially during times of stress, and they often result in the person behaving or communicating in an unusual, incoherent, or dysregulated manner (Cassidy & Shaver, 2016).

4.3 Attachment-Related Individual Differences from a Continuous-Dimensional Framework

So far, we have focused on describing attachment-related individual differences from a categorical-prototype framework. Next, we summarize them from a continuous-dimensional framework.

Within the latter, there are two continuous dimensions along which infant and adolescent/adult variations in attachment can be described – *avoidance* (of intimacy, dependence, and emotional expressiveness) and *anxiety* (about availability, responsivity, separation, abandonment, or insufficient care). Bartholomew and Horowitz (1991) proposed the avoidance dimension reflects how positive vs. negative the person's mental/neural representations of others are, whereas the anxiety dimension reflects how positive vs. negative the person's self-representations are. Hence, people with high *dismissing–avoidance* (positive views of others and self) exhibit higher avoidance and lower anxiety, people with high *fearful–avoidance* (positive views of others but a negative view of self) exhibit higher avoidance and anxiety, people with high *preoccupied* anxiety (negative views of themselves and others) exhibit lower avoidance but higher anxiety, and people with *secure attachment* (positive views of themselves and others) exhibit lower avoidance and anxiety (Mikulincer & Shaver, 2016). Within this framework, attachment security is defined more by what it is *not* than by what it *is*.

Most individual differences research using a continuous-dimensional approach has been conducted with adolescents and adults. These studies generally find that attachment anxiety is associated with lower self-esteem and self-efficacy, as well as with higher trait neuroticism (negative affectivity), general psychological distress, depression symptoms, anxiety symptoms, negative attentional bias, rejection sensitivity, behavioral inhibition, and couple violence behavior. Correspondingly, attachment avoidance is associated with lower self-disclosure, emotional expressiveness, support-seeking behavior, behavioral activation, and couple relationship commitment, as well as with higher emotional repression/suppression and distancing coping strategies (denial, distraction, disengagement, etc.). Both dimensions (anxiety and avoidance) are associated with lower perceived social support, conflict management skills, couple relationship intimacy, couple relationship satisfaction, and romantic-partner relationship satisfaction. Both dimensions are also related to higher loneliness, stronger tendency to escalate or withdraw from conflict, and greater recalled memories of negative parental behaviors during childhood (see Mikulincer & Shaver, 2016, for reviews).

4.4 An Integrated Conceptual Framework of Attachment-Related Individual Differences

Recently, Raby and colleagues (2021) developed a conceptual framework that integrates theoretical work (categorical-prototype and continuous-dimensional approaches), measurement strategies (behavioral, self-report, and narrative-based assessments), and empirical evidence (factor-analytic and taxometric) on attachment-related individual differences. Their integrated framework conceptualizes individual differences along two dimensions and categorizes attachment dispositions based on those dimensions. The first is *Relational Engagement vs. Avoidance*. The second is *Emotional Composure vs. Distress*. Individuals with higher Relational Avoidance and Emotional Distress can be described as exhibiting an *insecure–fearful-avoidant* disposition; those with higher Relational Avoidance and Emotional Composure, an *insecure–dismissing-avoidant* disposition; those with higher Relational Engagement and Emotional Distress, an *insecure–anxious/preoccupied* disposition; and those with higher Relational Engagement and Emotional Composure, a *secure* disposition. This integrated framework shows considerable promise, but because most existing attachment scholarship has used *either* the categorical-prototype approach *or* the continuous-dimensional approach, we use those approaches' language and conceptualizations in this Element.

4.5 Continuity and Variation in Attachment-Related Individual Differences

Before proceeding, we must discuss key nuances and complexities. People vary in how much continuity vs. variation they exhibit in their attachment-related functioning. We discuss two facets of this continuity and variation – across attachment relationships and across time.

4.5.1 Continuity and Variation across Different Attachment Relationships

Contrary to popularized notions of attachment, people do not just have a singular attachment style/disposition. Instead, they have a profile (constellation) of attachment dispositions/habits (and underlying constellation of mental/neural representations) that guide how they navigate the various attachment relationships in their lives. Sometimes these attachment dispositions/habits are quite similar – for example, they may have a secure attachment disposition when it comes to their relationships with their parents, peers, and romantic partner. Yet other times people can exhibit a quite different attachment disposition/habit in a particular relationship domain (e.g., an insecure–avoidant/dismissing disposition in romantic relationships but a secure attachment disposition with close friends) or with a particular person (e.g., an insecure–fearful-avoidant disposition with their mother but a secure disposition with their father). They may have a disorganized–unresolved attachment state of mind that gets elicited readily in certain relationships, situations, or contexts, yet otherwise they exhibit a stably organized attachment disposition – whether secure or not (Davis et al., 2021; Overall et al., 2003; Thompson et al., 2021).

Attachment scholars tend to understand these differences as reflecting idiographic profiles of attachment mental/neural representations (IWMs) that underlie idiographic profiles of attachment dispositions/habits. For example, at the broadest level of their mind/brain profile of attachment-related processing, people prototypically have an overarching (global) attachment representation of themselves, others, and themselves with others. These can be called global IWMs of self, others, and self-with-others. Like all attachment representations, these mental/neural representations are latent mental/neural structures; they are not directly observable or measurable. In contrast, like all attachment dispositions, people's global attachment disposition is partly manifest (via behavior, speech, etc.) and hence is directly observable and measurable. Indeed, many attachment measures purportedly assess a person's global attachment disposition/habit across their attachment relationships (Mikulincer & Shaver, 2016). We suggest calling this disposition/habit the person's *principal attachment*, which can be defined as the attachment disposition/habit that presently is most mentally/neurally dominant and chronically accessible (i.e., it is the most apt to become activated, given its frequency of usage, degree of overlearning, and extent of neuroconnectivity; Baldwin et al., 1996; Davis et al., 2021; Mikulincer & Shaver, 2023a) when the person experiences an actual or perceived threat to felt security.

At the secondary level of a person's mind/brain profile of attachment-related processing, they have developed a set of attachment representations and dispositions/habits for each major type of attachment relationship – child–parent/caregiver, other family members (siblings, grandparents, aunts/uncles, etc.), peers, romantic partners, and surrogate attachment figures (deities, pets, mentors). Finally, at the tertiary level of the person's mind/brain profile, they have developed a set of attachment representations and dispositions/habits for each specific attachment relationship, such as their relationship with their mother, father, stepmother, best friend, spouse/partner, pet(s), and God(s) (Davis et al., 2021; Overall et al., 2003).

As you can see, this understanding of attachment-related individual differences is more complex and nuanced than popularized notions of attachment suggest. Nonetheless, it makes conceptual sense that people vary in how they perceive and respond to different attachment figures. It also is more consistent with growing evidence that people's attachment dispositions across relationships are only modestly related (usually rs between .10 and .30; Baldwin et al., 1996; Fraley et al., 2011; Klohnen et al., 2005). In sum, someone's disposition to perceive and respond to one attachment figure probably shows only a slight resemblance to their disposition to perceive and respond to another attachment figure, and those dispositions may differ from one another more than they resemble each other. These dispositions/habits might also differ across different contexts (situations and settings) and across time. Next we discuss the latter.

4.5.2 Continuity and Variation across Time

There has been considerable research examining the continuity vs. variation of attachment dispositions over time, but most studies have *not* examined the same attachment-related construct using the same measurement method. Nevertheless, the best available meta-analytic evidence indicates that child–parent attachment dispositions and disorganization are modestly to moderately stable (a) during infancy and early childhood (Opie et al., 2021), (b) from infancy to late adolescence (Groh et al., 2014), and (c) from infancy to young adulthood (Fraley, 2002; Pinquart et al., 2013). Additionally, longitudinal evidence suggests adults' attachment dispositions to their parents are highly stable over time (test–retest rs of .80 or higher over periods ranging from a few weeks to 1 year). By comparison, adults' romantic attachment disposition is quite stable in the short-term (rs ≈ .70) but is much less stable over the longer-term (rs ≈ .30 over 1 year; Fraley et al., 2011). The continuity vs. variation of other types of attachment-related individual differences (peer, best-friend, and R/S attachment) is unknown.

4.6 Determinants of Attachment-Related Individual Differences

Research indicates the main determinant of secure vs. insecure/disorganized attachment is attachment figures' reliable *caregiving sensitivity* – their "ability to notice, interpret, and quickly respond to [the care-seeking person's] signals of need and/or interest" (Madigan et al., 2023, p. 839). Basically, what helps people develop a secure attachment disposition is when their attachment figures (e.g., primary caregivers during early childhood; peers and romantic partners during adolescence and adulthood) are reliably sensitive, available, and responsive (to their needs and their efforts to connect relationally). The more often their attachment figures respond in these ways, the more consolidated a secure attachment disposition becomes (Granqvist, 2020; Thompson et al., 2021).

Contemporary theory and research suggest additional factors contribute to the development of a secure (vs. insecure/disorganized) attachment. In parent–child relationships, one key factor is the parental *caregiver's own attachment disposition/representations*, given that parental caregivers tend to transmit their own attachment disposition/representations to their offspring (via what is called *intergenerational transmission*; Verhage et al., 2016). In attachment relationships more broadly, the caregiver's *reflective functioning* may play a role – their ability "to understand and interpret – implicitly and explicitly – one's own and others' behavior as an expression of mental states such as feelings, thoughts, fantasies, beliefs, and desires" (Katznelson, 2014, p. 108). Another influential determinant may be the relational context's *autonomy support* – the degree to which the attachment relationship's context is characterized by caregiving behaviors and environmental conditions that foster the attached person's sense of autonomy, thereby facilitating intrinsic motivation and the internalization of security-enhancing caregiving (Mikulincer & Shaver, 2004; Ryan & Deci, 2000). Other potentially influential factors for developing a secure attachment disposition include *contextual facilitative conditions*, *caregiver warmth* and *limit-setting*, and *relational attunement* and *synchrony* (van IJzendoorn & Bakermans-Kranenburg, 2019). Relational attunement and synchrony are especially key determinants of secure attachment in the reciprocal-caregiving relationships of adolescence and adulthood, namely close friendships and romantic partnerships (Cassidy & Shaver, 2016; Mikulincer & Shaver, 2016).

Lastly, there is growing evidence that *patterns of nature–nurture interaction* (gene x environment and epigenetic effects) influence the development of secure vs. insecure or disorganized attachment (Dugan et al., 2025; Erkoreka et al., 2021). For example, there likely are susceptibility genes that make individuals differentially susceptible to certain positive or adverse environmental influences, making their development of a secure attachment disposition respectively more or less likely. Of note, family-shared environmental influences (the caregiver, caregiving relationship, and surrounding environmental conditions) seem to have a larger influence on the development of a secure attachment disposition during infancy (Cassidy & Shaver, 2016). The influence of genetic and nonshared-environmental influences seems to increase over time, such that between 36% and 45% of the variability in adolescent and adult attachment dispositions/habits may be explained by genetics (Dugan et al., 2025; Erkoreka et al., 2021; Fearon et al., 2014).[2]

---

[2] This level of heritability (genetic influence) is similar to that of well-being (36%; Bartels, 2015), life satisfaction (32%; Bartels, 2015), personality traits (40%; Mõttus et al., 2025; Vukasović & Bratko, 2015), and major depression (37%; Sullivan et al., 2000). However, such percentages apply to phenotypic variation among twins (and in some studies, adoptees) so cannot automatically be generalized to nontwin populations. Hence, these percentages should be taken with a considerable grain of salt. Moreover, the development of complex phenotypes like these is most likely a function of nature–nurture transactions operating over time and situations (i.e., genes x environment, not genes + environment; Granqvist, 2020).

4.7 Clarifications and Caveats

The notion of individual differences in attachment flows seamlessly from the normative tenets of attachment theory, especially Bowlby's descriptions of IWMs. Perhaps partly for that reason, many people assume that attachment-related individual differences are what is most important about attachment and, consequently, that secure attachment is a prerequisite for healthy human development. That is simply not the case. What is most important is that children, adolescents, and young adults get safe, stable, and shared care from their caregivers (Forslund et al., 2022; van IJzendoorn & Bakermans-Kranenburg, 2024).

The reader may recall that roughly 50% of children develop insecure attachment with a given caregiver, and many of these children develop reasonably well. Furthermore, most caregivers of insecurely attached children love their children dearly and hope for their children's best outcomes. They feed, protect, and care for their children in many important ways, even if – on average – they may provide somewhat less-sensitive caregiving than caregivers of children with a principal secure attachment can offer. Correspondingly, most insecurely attached children love their caregivers, protest against separation from them, and mourn their loss.

Consequently, it is unsurprising that research on developmental sequelae of attachment usually finds that only small to moderate effect sizes can be attributed solely to attachment-related individual differences. Human development is extremely complex, involving many important components beyond attachment generally and attachment-related individual differences specifically. Single factors rarely explain much variation in development on their own, even if they make meaningful contributions alongside other factors.

We make these clarifying remarks not to dismiss attachment-related individual differences from consideration but to prevent oversimplifications, caricatures, exaggerations, and misapplications (Forslund et al., 2022; Granqvist et al., 2017; van IJzendoorn & Bakermans-Kranenburg, 2024). Such oversimplifications have increasingly emerged in recent years – especially in applied and popular press literatures – and they sometimes have had tragic consequences. In a few countries, some children have been removed from their caregivers *solely* because social authorities have estimated – via poorly validated attachment measures – that these children have insecure attachment dispositions toward their caregivers (Granqvist, 2016). Unfortunately, permanent or repeated removals of children from their caregivers are likely to have more seriously negative effects on child development than a principal insecure attachment disposition does – presuming that children with a principal insecure attachment enjoy safe, stable, and shared care, as many do. It should be noted here that Bowlby's species-typical theory was originally founded to explain the severely adverse effects of prolonged, repeated separations from caregivers.

4.8 Conclusion

In Section 4, we have described the three main patterns of attachment (secure, insecure–avoidant/dismissing, and insecure–resistant/preoccupied) identified by Ainsworth and Main, along with the fourth form of attachment – disorganized–disoriented/unresolved – identified by Main and Solomon (1990). We considered the developmental origins and sequelae of attachment-related individual differences. Finally, we concluded that even if a focus on individual differences has almost come to define attachment research, the topic of attachment is far broader than individual differences. At the same time, attachment-related individual differences are important to consider, when it comes both to human and R/S attachment. Sections 5 and 6 will explore the ways these individual differences develop and manifest in people's perceived attachment relationships with supernatural figures such as God.

5 The Correspondence Facets of Human Attachment and Religion/Spirituality

"It is easier to build strong children than to repair broken men [and women]."
– Fredrick Douglass (n.d.), an American abolitionist, writer, orator, and social reformer

Two major hypotheses have come to characterize research and theory on how individual differences in human attachment security (vs. insecurity/disorganization) are linked to variations in facets of R/S beliefs, behaviors, experiences, and functioning. Historically, these have been labeled the "correspondence" and "compensation" hypotheses (Kirkpatrick, 2005). For reasons we will discuss, we refer to them as the correspondence and compensation *facets*. Section 5 focuses on the former, and Section 6 focuses on the latter.

Section 5 has four parts. First, we summarize the history and evolution of the correspondence and compensation ideas. Second, we clarify distinctions between two facets of correspondence – (a) the correspondence of attachment-based mental/neural representations ("internal working model [IWM]" correspondence) and (b) the correspondence of internalized social–cultural learning ("socialized" correspondence). Third, empirical research on these two facets of correspondence is reviewed. Finally, we provide historical case examples illustrating these facets and their possible valences. The first example illustrates the development and manifestation of secure human and R/S attachment dispositions via social–cultural learning (socialized correspondence) and internalized representations of reliably security-enhancing caregiving (security-based IWM correspondence). The second example illustrates the development and manifestation of insecure/disorganized human and R/S attachment (insecurity-based IWM correspondence), including elements of socialized correspondence.

5.1 History and Evolution of the Correspondence and Compensation Ideas

The correspondence and compensation hypotheses were first proposed by psychologists Kirkpatrick (1992, 2005) and Shaver (Kirkpatrick & Shaver, 1990, 1992). These hypotheses were originally framed as competing models to explain how individual differences in human attachment relate to people's religiousness/spirituality generally and perceived relationship with God(s) specifically. Based on Bowlby's (1973) concept of IWMs becoming generalized across relationships, the original correspondence hypothesis predicted that the attachment representations and dispositions/habits people develop in their human attachment relationships become generalized onto the attachment representations and dispositions/habits they develop in perceived relationship with God(s). If someone develops a secure attachment disposition with humans (including secure IWMs of self, others, and self-with-others), they most likely will develop a secure attachment disposition with God(s) (including secure IWMs of self, God[s], and self-with-God[s]). If they develop an insecure (and/or disorganized) attachment with humans (including insecure and/or disorganized/incoherent IWMs of self, others, and self-with-others), they will most likely develop an insecure (and/or disorganized) attachment with God(s).

The original compensation hypothesis was based on Ainsworth's (1985) notion that surrogate attachment figures function psychologically as surrogates (replacements) for inadequate human attachment figures. It posited that people with insecure (and/or disorganized) attachment may develop a surrogate relationship with God(s) – regardless of whether their perceived relationship with God is ultimately secure or insecure – because this surrogate relationship can help them compensate emotionally for their insecure (and/or disorganized) human attachment (see Section 6).

After these original hypotheses were proposed, studies began revealing evidence supporting them both, sometimes from the same dataset. For example, supporting the compensation hypothesis, Kirkpatrick and Shaver (1990) found that adults who reported an insecure–avoidant/dismissing *maternal* attachment history reported the highest levels of intrinsic religiousness, loving God representations, and belief in a personal God with whom they had a relationship, relative to adults who reported a secure or insecure–resistant/preoccupied maternal attachment history.[3] Yet, from the same dataset, Kirkpatrick and Shaver (1992) found that adults who had a secure *romantic* attachment disposition reported having the highest religious commitment and most positive/loving God representations, relative to adults with insecure–avoidant/dismissing and insecure–resistant/preoccupied attachment. In short, Kirkpatrick and Shaver's (1990) results supported the compensation hypothesis, yet Kirkpatrick and Shaver's (1992) results from the same dataset supported the correspondence hypothesis.

One reason that evidence for both hypotheses began amassing was that the original formulation of them as "competing" was scientifically problematic. Falsifiability – the possibility that empirical observations can demonstrate a theory is inaccurate – is a core criterion for respectable scientific inquiry (Popper, 1962/2014). However, these jointly presented "competing" attachment-based hypotheses meant virtually any empirical finding on human–R/S attachment (except null results) would confirm attachment-theory predictions. Theoretical refinement was needed (Granqvist, 2020).

Hence, building on findings from early studies (Granqvist, 1998; Kirkpatrick & Shaver, 1990), Granqvist and Hagekull (1999) proposed the *socialized correspondence hypothesis*. It revised the original correspondence hypothesis by adding a moderator (qualifying variable) to it – caregiver religiousness/spirituality. The socialized correspondence hypothesis posited there are two levels (facets) of correspondence – one at the level of relationally internalized attachment security (generalized secure IWMs of self, others, and self-with-others) and one at the level of socially/culturally internalized religiousness/spirituality (a general R/S worldview orientation to life). Specifically, it posited that when caregivers (a) provide their offspring with sensitive caregiving/secure attachment and (b) do so within a family and/or cultural environment that is highly R/S, then the child likely will (c) adopt an R/S worldview orientation to life, (d) develop a principal secure attachment disposition (with secure/coherent underlying IWMs of self, others, and self-with-others), and (e) develop a secure attachment disposition with God(s), including secure/coherent underlying IWMs of self, God, and self-with-God(s) (Granqvist, 2020).

Over the past two decades, evidence supporting the IWM correspondence, socialized correspondence, and compensation hypotheses has continued amassing (Granqvist, 2020; Granqvist & Kirkpatrick, 2016). Thankfully, theorizing

---

[3] Importantly, this pattern was only observed among participants who had grown up with mothers low in religiousness.

on the complex, context-dependent relations between individual differences in human and R/S attachment has evolved as well (Granqvist, 2020; Hall et al., 2009). We propose these three "hypotheses" can now be integrated into a unified conceptual framework that recognizes the validity and utility of each. All three are potential *facets* for describing how individual differences in human attachment, religion/spirituality, and R/S attachment can develop and manifest.

Hence, there are three *facets* of human–R/S attachment functioning. One facet focuses on corresponding attachment representations and dispositions/habits (*IWM correspondence*). Another emphasizes social-cultural learning of an R/S (or non-R/S) worldview, typically in the context of sensitive caregiving and secure attachment (*socialized correspondence*). The third centers on attachment representations and dispositions that compensate emotionally either for enduring habits of attachment insecurity/disorganization or for situationally salient states of attachment insecurity (e.g., times of heightened attachment-related distress, such as situations of significant loss, grief, separation, transition, or uncertainty; *emotional compensation*). Notably, the extent to which any one of these facets characterizes a given individual's religion/spirituality varies. For some individuals, IWM and socialized correspondence are both highly relevant (e.g., a person feeling a secure attachment to God who was raised by religious and *sensitive* caregivers). For others, one of these facets applies more so than the other (e.g., a person who feels insecure with God but who was raised by religious, *insensitive* caregivers). In Sections 5 and 6, we will also see examples (e.g., Abraham Lincoln) of how IWM correspondence and socialized correspondence may co-occur with emotional compensation.

5.2 Clarifications about IWM and Socialized Correspondence

Because both the IWM and socialized correspondence ideas focus on attachment-based correspondence, some clarifications about them are warranted. In principle, these two facets can be distinguished conceptually, but in practice they are usually inter-related. Social–cultural learning influences the ways IWMs develop, manifest, and change. Likewise, the IWMs people develop shape how they interact with their social–cultural surroundings, which influences the social ecology in which they are embedded. Regardless, it is helpful to understand some conceptual and pragmatic distinctions between IWM and socialized correspondence.

IWM correspondence essentially refers to the development and manifestation of attachment-based mental/neural representations that are formed through human relationships and then generalize onto a person's religion/spirituality, including their perceived relationship with God(s). See Figure 1 for a visual

Two Forms of the Internal Working Model (IWM) Correspondence Facet

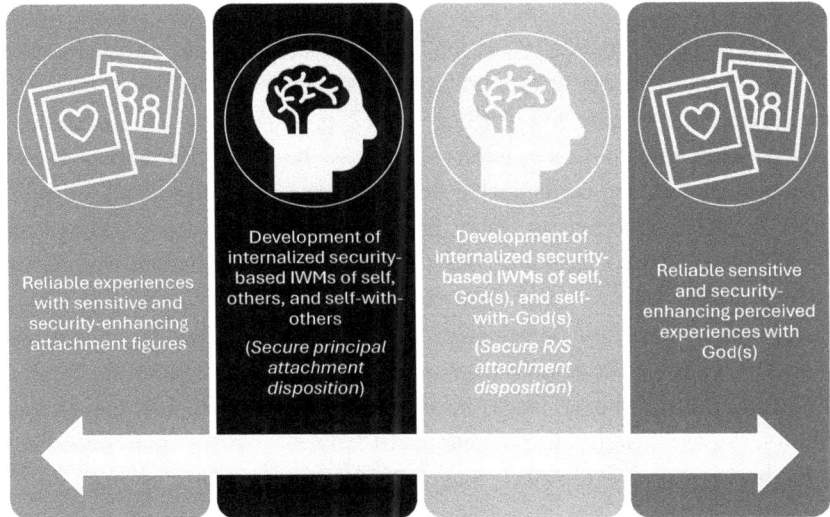

(a) Security-based IWM correspondence

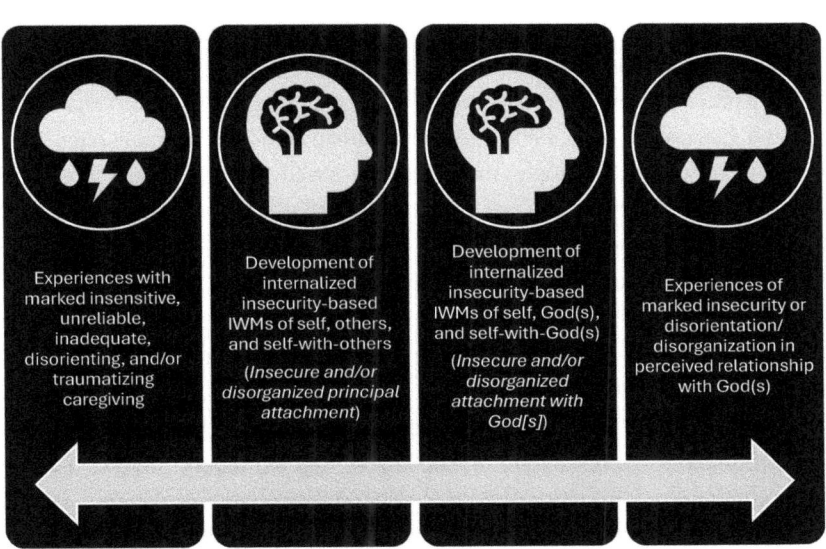

(b) Insecurity-based IWM correspondence

Figure 1 Two forms of the internal working model (IWM) correspondence facet
(a) Security-based IWM correspondence
(b) Insecurity-based IWM correspondence

depiction. *Mental representations* are the "cognitive structures that reflect acquired knowledge and experience, and that provide the material on which cognitive processes operate" (Carlston, 2010, p. 39), and *neural representations* are "a pattern of neural firing that represents something, such as a memory, bodily sensation, or perception" (Siegel, 2012, p. 479). We often refer collectively to mental/neural representations, because the *mind* ("an embodied and relational process that regulates the flow of energy and information," Siegel, 2020, p. 507) and brain (or, more precisely, the extended nervous system throughout the body) represent two interrelated sides of human experience (Siegel, 2020). Mental/neural representations are the pathways along which energy and information flow inside a person, shaping their psychophysiological–R/S experience at a given moment. These representations are formed and changed through experiences in *relationships*, which are how energy and information are shared and communicated between two or more perceived living beings (Davis et al., 2021; Siegel, 2020).

Taken together, IWM correspondence refers to how experiences in human relationships lead to the development of experience-based mental/neural representations that not only guide a person's biopsychosocial experiences in human relationships but also guide their biopsychosocial–R/S experiences in perceived relationship with God(s). For people who develop and manifest correspondent positive (security-based) IWMs in their human and R/S relationships, they prototypically have developed these security-based mental/neural representations through reliably sensitive and security-enhancing caregiving in their human relationships (e.g., with early caregivers, peers, romantic partners, etc.). Then, via generalizing mental/neural representations of self, others, and relationships (self-with-others), they develop and manifest generally positive (security-based) mental/neural representations of God(s) and of themselves in relationship with God(s). This type of IWM correspondence can be called *security-based IWM correspondence* (see Figure 1a).

Unfortunately, as discussed in Section 4, approximately 50% of people develop negative (insecurity-based and/or disorganized/incoherent) IWMs through experiences in their human relationships, typically due to marked insensitive, unreliable, inadequate, disorienting, and/or traumatizing caregiving (Bakermans-Kranenburg et al., 2024; Madigan et al., 2023). Via a correspondent IWM-generalizing process, these individuals might develop and manifest generally negative mental/neural representations of God(s) and of themselves in relationship with God(s). This type of IWM correspondence can be called *insecurity-based IWM correspondence* (see Figure 1b).

Like IWM correspondence, socialized correspondence (see Figure 2) fundamentally refers to the internalization of experiences – in this case internalized

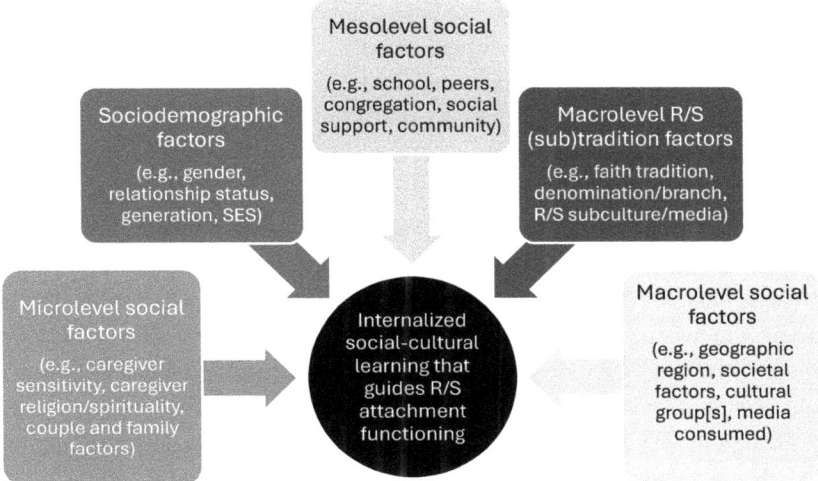

Figure 2 The socialized correspondence facet

Note: SES = socioeconomic status; R/S = religious/spiritual.

social–cultural learning experiences. Naturally, socialized correspondence centers on the internalizing process of *socialization*, defined as "the way in which individuals are assisted in becoming members of one or more social groups . . . . [and] involves a variety of outcomes, including the acquisition of rules, roles, standards, and values across the social, emotional, cognitive, and personal domains" (Grusec & Hastings, 2015, p. xi). When it comes to attachment and religion/spirituality, this socialization process initially occurs through influences from primary caregivers (see Section 3). Through explicit communication (e.g., verbal instruction) and implicit communication (e.g., social modeling), a child's caregivers usually socialize their children into adopting the same R/S or non-R/S beliefs, practices, standards, and values they hold. Whether intentional or not, socialization might only be "successful" if the caregiver provides reliably sensitive caregiving, such that the child develops a principal secure attachment disposition. If so, then via social–(cultural) learning, the securely attached child often develops a socially (culturally) corresponding approach to religion/spirituality generally and God(s) specifically. If their caregiver(s) exhibited R/S beliefs and behaviors, potentially including a secure R/S attachment disposition toward God(s), the child likely develops corresponding forms of religiousness/spirituality and a secure attachment with God. Conversely, if the caregiver(s) exhibited a non-R/S (e.g., atheist or agnostic) worldview (and hence no relationship with God[s]), the securely attached child likely develops a correspondingly non-R/S worldview and no attachment relationship with

God(s). In Section 6, we will see what happens for children who initially develop a principal insecure or disorganized attachment.

As children mature and interact with others beyond their primary caregivers, socialized correspondence can reflect several social–cultural influences besides their childhood caregivers' influence. This is particularly the case as the individual moves through adolescence, into young adulthood, and beyond. These socialization vehicles can include siblings, extended family members (especially in collectivistic cultures), peer groups, best friends, romantic partners, teachers, mentors, R/S leaders, and public figures. They also can include larger social systems such as neighborhoods, communities, congregations, cultural groups, societies, institutions (schools, workplaces), and religious (sub)traditions (denominations, branches, sects). Media and generational influences can play a significant socializing role as well (Grusec & Hastings, 2015). If applicable, the relative influence of any of these nonparental socializing agents might be amplified for a person who is securely attached to that agent, or it might be suppressed if a person is insecurely attached to that agent.

5.3 Research on IWM and Socialized Correspondence

Many studies have supported the positively valenced IWM correspondence facet by which secure human attachment representations, dispositions, and functioning are linked to secure R/S attachment representations, dispositions, and functioning. For instance, cross-sectional studies with US undergraduates (Hall et al., 2009; Kirkpatrick, 1998), Italian Catholic priests (Cassibba et al., 2008), and Italian mother–child dyads (Cassibba et al., 2013) have found that people with a current secure attachment disposition (and underlying positive IWMs of self and others) often concurrently display a secure R/S attachment disposition (and positive IWMs of self and God).

The inverse finding has emerged for people who display insecure attachment dispositions/habits or representations. Reflecting insecure/disorganized IWM correspondence, youth and adults who exhibit insecure/disorganized attachment with their parents or romantic partners (and negative or incoherent IWMs of self and/or others) tend to exhibit insecure/disorganized R/S attachment (and negative or incoherent IWMs of self and God). This finding has emerged in studies of Italian mother–child dyads (Cassibba et al., 2013), Turkish Muslim adults (Kıraç, 2021), US married heterosexual couples (Pollard et al., 2014), Polish Catholic adults (Zarzycka, 2019), and US Christian young adults (Hall et al., 2009; Sandage et al., 2015).

Both valences of IWM correspondence have been replicated in experimental studies as well. Birgegard and Granqvist (2004) found that, when faced with a subliminal attachment-activating cue, Swedish Christian adults who had memories of a secure attachment history with their parents responded to God securely – by turning *toward* God (e.g., engaging in proximity-seeking behavior). Conversely, those who recalled an insecure parental attachment history responded to God insecurely – by turning *away* from God. Similar security-based and insecurity-based IWM correspondence has been found in experimental studies with school-aged children in Sweden (Granqvist et al., 2007b) and with Jewish adults in Israel (Granqvist et al., 2012b).

Regarding socialized correspondence, many studies have revealed evidence supporting its main tenet – that children who receive sensitive caregiving from R/S caregivers will develop and manifest caregiver-corresponding religiousness/spirituality, including secure human and R/S attachment representations/functioning. This finding has emerged with community adults in the United States (Kirkpatrick & Shaver, 1990, 1992), undergraduates in Sweden (Granqvist, 1998; Granqvist & Hagekull, 1999), charismatic Christians in Sweden (Lehmivaara & Granqvist, 2025), and adolescent–caregiver dyads in the United States (Kim-Spoon et al., 2012).

Scientific studies have found evidence that these and other socializing agents can contribute to internalized social–cultural learning correspondence in R/S attachment functioning. So far, research has identified at least five types of socializing influences:

- microlevel social factors (e.g., caregiving sensitivity [Granqvist et al., 2007a]; parent–child attachment security [Kim-Spoon et al., 2012]; and living conditions [Codato et al., 2011; Goodman et al., 2022]),
- sociodemographic factors (e.g., gender identity [Jung, 2020]; romantic relationship status [Granqvist & Hagekull, 2000, 2003]),
- mesolevel social factors (e.g., neighborhood-level religiosity [Maimon & Kuhl, 2008]),
- macrolevel R/S (sub)tradition factors (e.g., Judaism [Kaplan et al., 2012]; Islam [Abu-Rayya et al., 2016]; Christian denomination/subgroup [Lehmivaara & Granqvist, 2025]), and
- macrolevel social factors (e.g., geographic region [Vonk et al., 2019]).

5.4 Case Examples

5.4.1 Anne Frank: Security-Based IWM Correspondence and Socialized Correspondence

Anne Frank (1929–1945) is one of the world's youngest and most beloved authors. Her *Diary of a Young Girl*, chronicling 2 years of hiding during the

Holocaust, has inspired generations. It begins 4 weeks before her family and a few others went into hiding in a secret annex of her father's office building. It ends 3 days before they were discovered and transported to concentration camps. Only Anne's father survived (Anne Frank House, 2025).

Based on Anne's diary and other records, Anne seems to have had a principal secure attachment disposition. She had a close, loving relationship with her father, and both her parents provided reliably sensitive caregiving. Anne was consistently able to make and keep friends, even amid the stressful circumstances of economic uncertainty and rising antisemitism in her earliest years and the major adjustment of emigrating from Germany to Holland at age 4. Throughout her short life, Anne exhibited a security and autonomy of thought, behavior, and expression that was remarkable given her culture, age, and circumstances. She was a curious, courageous, outspoken, optimistic, lively, insightful, humorous, strong-willed, and self-motivated girl. She apparently internalized security-based IWMs of herself, others, and herself in relationship with others (Müller, 2013).

Anne's mother was a religiously educated, orthodox, and observant Jew, and her father was a religiously liberal and less-observant Jew. Anne's parents allowed Anne considerable autonomy in developing her unique expression of Jewish religion/spirituality. Anne was not particularly R/S before going into hiding, but as commonly happens under stressful circumstances (see Section 6), her faith and relationship with God deepened during those 2 years. Perhaps mainly because of the strength of her secure attachment to her father, Anne's religion/spirituality came to resemble her father's religion/spirituality more than her mother's. Anne's views of God were more benevolent, inclusive, expansive, character-oriented, nature-incorporative, and relationally focused than her mother's, which seemed more reverently fearful, punishment-avoidant, commandment-oriented, and duty-focused. Anne viewed and related with God as a strong, loving attachment figure who knew and loved her deeply, helped her live morally, always protected and delivered her and the Jewish people, and steadfastly breathed hope, joy, and courage into her soul (Frank, 1947/2023; Müller, 2013).

Even after living in hiding a year and a half, Anne maintained this buoyant spirit. In her March 7, 1944, entry, she shared: "I lie in bed at night, after ending my prayers with the words 'I thank you, God, for all that is Good and Dear and Beautiful,' and I'm filled with joy" (Frank, 1947/2023, p. 211). A month later, she shared a poignant anthem that reverberated with social learning she had internalized from her mother's cherished Jewish heritage and her father's resilient faith that God and goodness always prevail:

"We've been strongly reminded of the fact that we're Jews in chains, chained to one spot, without any rights, but with a thousand obligations. We must put our feelings aside; we must be brave and strong, bear discomfort without complaint, do whatever is in our power and trust in God. One day this terrible war will be over. The time will come when we'll be people again and not just Jews! . . . .

There will be a way out. God has never deserted our people. Through the ages Jews have had to suffer, but through the ages they've gone on living, and the centuries of suffering have only made them stronger." (Frank, 1947/2023, p. 261)[4]

5.4.2 Abraham Lincoln: Insecurity-Based IWM Correspondence and Socialized Correspondence

Historians and the public almost universally agree Abraham Lincoln was the greatest US President, citing his exemplary leadership during the American Civil War, his pivotal role in ending US slavery, and his inspiring vision for global liberalism and human equality. Yet Lincoln's life was marked by tremendous suffering, loss, and grief. His infant brother died when Lincoln was 3 years old, his beloved mother died when Lincoln was 9, and his other sibling (and best friend) died when he was 19. Ann Rutledge – his dear friend and likely first love – died when Lincoln was 26. Furthermore, his courtship, broken-off engagement, and eventual marriage to Mary Todd were fraught with emotional turbulence and reciprocal attachment insecurity, fueled by each partner's chronic mental health difficulties. Abraham struggled with recurrent, persistent, and sometimes suicidal depression, and his wife Mary Todd struggled with bipolar disorder (recurrent manic and depressive episodes), complicated grief, and likely borderline personality disorder (with histrionic features). Moreover, the Lincolns suffered the tragic loss of several loved ones, including their young son "Eddie" at age 4 and their third son "Willie" at age 11. These losses and stressors are compounded by the financial and social stressors that Lincoln faced throughout his life, along with the political, legal, public opinion, and military stressors he endured during adulthood (Mansfield, 2012; White, 2009).

The evolution of Lincoln's attachment patterns and religion/spirituality are every bit as complex and multifaceted as he was. Lincoln had a close and secure attachment relationship with his mother. She was a kind, loving, and sensitive caregiver who was a devout Christian. Her tragic, sudden loss (due to a fast-acting

---

[4] Countless other historical figures seem to have exhibited security-based IWM correspondence, based on historical evidence. These include Martin Luther King, Jr., Billy Graham, Elisabeth Elliot, Malala Yousafzai, Elie Wiesel, Nelson Mandela, Joni Eareckson Tada, Pope John Paul II, and Corrie ten Boom.

disease that caused horrifying, convulsive vomiting) was traumatizing to 9-year-old Lincoln, who watched her die over a few days and rarely spoke about her or her death after that. This traumatizing loss may have led Lincoln to develop a principal disorganized–disoriented/unresolved attachment by the time of adolescence. He seemingly developed a secondary insecure–avoidant/dismissing attachment by then as well, probably due to his emotionally distant and insensitive relationship with his father Thomas, who was a rageful, unpredictable, demanding, critical, and physically violent man and whom Lincoln long despised. In fact, it is possible Thomas Lincoln exhibited a similar attachment classification as Abraham, given that Thomas witnessed his own father's murder by Native Americans when he was 8 years old and subsequently grew up under difficult, survival-oriented life conditions (Mansfield, 2012; White, 2009). Intergenerational transmission of unresolved loss and disorganized attachment – a well-documented psychological phenomenon (Cassidy & Shaver, 2016) – probably affected Abraham Lincoln's religion/spirituality as well.

Until his mother's death when Lincoln was 9, Lincoln received strong Christian socialization through his mother's modeling of Christian character and her sharing of Bible stories. However, once she passed, Lincoln's R/S socialization took a sharp turn. His exposure to Christianity was then limited to family attendance at religious services at their local Separatist Baptist church (which emphasized predestination and heavy-handed legalism) and at itinerant camp/revivalist meetings (which were common on the western US frontier, drew huge interdenominational Christian crowds, and were characterized by melodramatic sermons and audience responses). After both types of services, Lincoln would often get up on a stump and reenact a sermon – recited nearly word-for-word and hilariously "performed" using the preacher's caricatured voice and mannerisms. Lincoln's irate father eventually forbade it (Mansfield, 2012).

At age 22, a year after helping his father and stepmother move to Illinois, Lincoln moved to start a life of his own. Lincoln's despisal of his father and his father's legalistic, melodramatic Christianity intensified. Through voraciously consuming works by Enlightenment-era, anti-Christian minds (like Robert Burns, Thomas Paine, Edward Gibbon, and C.F. Volney), Lincoln came to believe God did not exist, that the Bible was a myth and an uninspired human book full of contradictions, and that Jesus Christ was "a bastard" and not the Son of God. Lincoln's anti-Christian beliefs and vitriol became so well-known that he gained a widespread reputation as an "infidel." The anti-Christian public comments Lincoln made during this phase cost him personally and politically for a long time (Mansfield, 2012).

Historians are unsure whether the "angry atheism" of Lincoln's 20s and 30s was mainly fueled by his hatred of his father, his despisal of self-righteous Christian preachers, or his rage against God for the unremitting suffering he had endured.

Regarding the latter, Lincoln was notoriously closed-lipped about his childhood but later confided in his friend and law partner: "My mother was a bastard [and] the daughter of a nobleman ... of Virginia" (Mansfield, 2012, p. 1). Ashamed of his origins, throughout life, Lincoln always thought he was cursed, that "God had forsaken him" (Mansfield, 2012, p. 44), and that he was left to suffer alone because of the sins of his ancestors. It was not until his late 30s that Lincoln's struggles with his own soul and the soul of the American nation led to an R/S transformation that personalized a blend of his mother's Christian faith with an Enlightenment evolution of it (Mansfield, 2012). This type of transformation from insecurity-based R/S attachment to compensatory R/S attachment is the topic to which we will turn in Section 6, and we will revisit Lincoln's R/S journey along the way.

5.5 Conclusion

Section 5 examined how individual differences in human attachment security and R/S socialization correspond to people's R/S beliefs and behaviors. The original correspondence hypothesis, developed by Kirkpatrick and Shaver, suggested the attachment patterns people developed in human relationships get generalized onto their perceived relationship with God – secure human attachment typically leads to secure R/S attachment, whereas insecure (and/or disorganized) human attachment usually corresponds to insecure (and/or disorganized) R/S attachment. Granqvist and Hagekull refined the framework by proposing socialized correspondence, which added caregiver religiousness/spirituality as a moderating factor. This revision recognized two facets of correspondence: IWM correspondence (involving generalized attachment representations) and socialized correspondence (involving internalized social–cultural learning of religious worldviews). This integrated framework therefore treats these as two complementary facets of correspondence. IWM correspondence focuses on how attachment-based mental/neural representations from human relationships generalize onto divine attachment relationships. Socialized correspondence emphasizes how children internalize caregivers' R/S (or non-R/S) beliefs and practices through socialization processes, particularly if they received sensitive caregiving. Extensive empirical research supports both these facets of correspondence, demonstrating their validity as processes for understanding the complex relationships between human attachment and R/S functioning.

6 The Compensation Facet of Human Attachment and Religion/Spirituality

> "You may trod me in the very dirt / But still, like dust, I'll rise ....
> Up from a past that's rooted in pain / I rise."
> – Maya Angelou (1978, pp. 41–42)

People can draw on an attachment relationship with God(s) for all sorts of reasons – safety and security (Granqvist & Kirkpatrick, 2016), need and wish fulfillment (Davis et al., 2023; Freud, 1953–1974), and social (e.g., familial) and cultural entraining (Granqvist, 2020; Norenzayan et al., 2016). The compensation facet of human attachment and religion/spirituality focuses on the process by which people draw on religion/spirituality, often including a perceived relationship with God(s), to compensate emotionally either (a) for insecure and/or disorganized attachment dispositions/habits and strategies or (b) for situationally based mental/neural states of heightened attachment insecurity. The latter can include situations involving chronic stress, pain, illness, uncertainty, transition, adjustment, loss, or grief (Granqvist, 2020).

Section 5 described the origins of the compensation "hypothesis," so Section 6 begins by exploring contemporary theorizing on the compensation facet of human attachment and R/S functioning. Next, we summarize empirical research on its two forms – dispositional and situational emotional compensation. Finally, we illustrate these with case examples.

6.1 Contemporary Theorizing on the Compensation Facet

Originally, the compensation "hypothesis" focused on people with insecure (and/or disorganized attachment), positing they utilized religion/spirituality and their relationship with God(s) to function as a psychological surrogate (replacement) for the suboptimal human caregiving they received during childhood (Kirkpatrick, 2005; cf. Ainsworth, 1985). Based on advancements in theory and research on attachment, religion/spirituality, and R/S attachment, it now is clear that a wide variety of people utilize religion/spirituality (including a perceived relationship with God) to compensate emotionally for dispositional or situational attachment insecurity. This includes people who do or do not have (a) an insecure/disorganized attachment history, (b) an insecure/disorganized current attachment, (c) an R/S childhood history, or (d) a current R/S affiliation or worldview. In short, the compensation facet of human attachment and religion/spirituality is now more widely applicable and situationally inclusive.

The compensation facet can now be more conceptually precise as well. We propose the following reformulation. Based on Mikulincer and Shaver's (2003, 2016) empirically supported model of attachment-system activation and functioning (Figure 3), we posit that people often utilize religion/spirituality and/or a relationship with God(s) to compensate emotionally at times when an external or internalized human attachment figure is perceived as unavailable, unresponsive, insensitive, or otherwise incapable of offering needed caregiving. The person can then ideally draw on religion/spirituality and/or God(s) to help

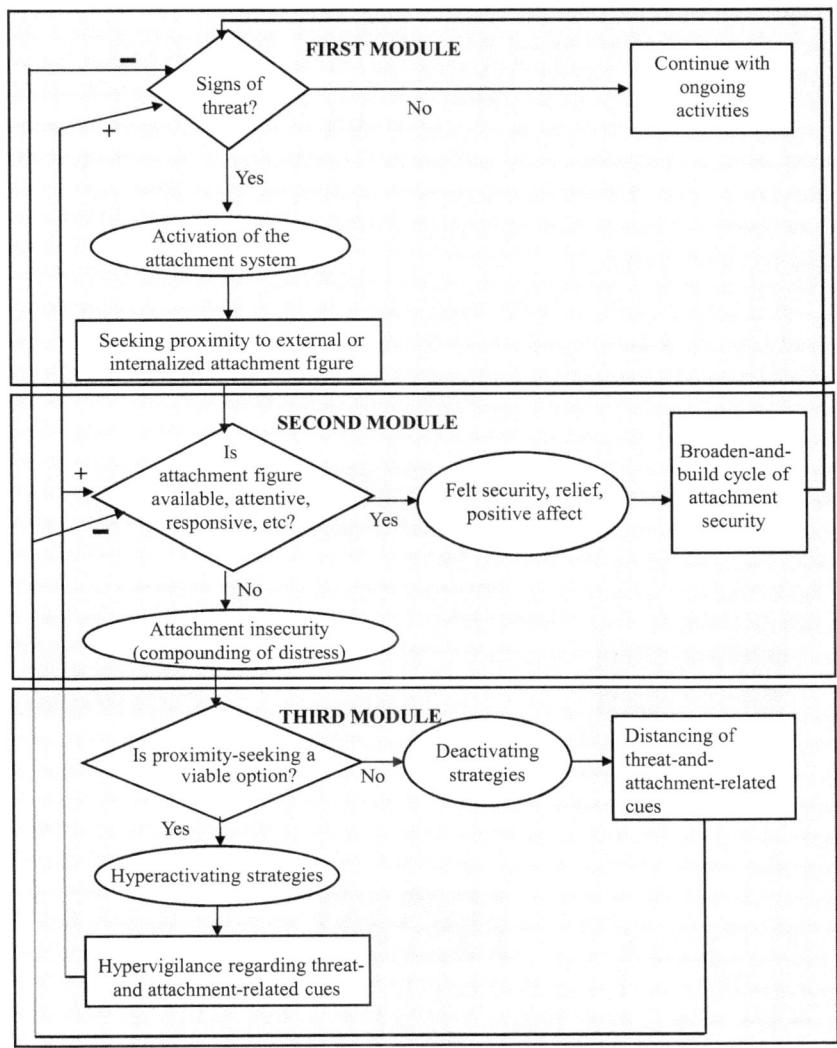

Figure 3 Mikulincer and shaver's (2003, 2016) model of attachment-system activation and functioning

Reprinted from *Attachment in Adulthood: Structure, Dynamics, and Change* (2nd ed., p. 51), by Mario Mikulincer and Phillip Shaver, 2016, Guilford Press. Copyright 2016 by Guilford Press. Reprinted with permission.

restore a sense of felt security, deactivate the attachment system, and return to nonattachment activities (top part of Figure 3's second and first modules). If they cannot, they experience compounded attachment insecurity, leading them to engage in deactivating (insecure–avoidant/dismissing), hyperactivating (insecure–anxious/preoccupied), or chaotic (disorganized–disoriented) strategies of human or R/S attachment (second and third modules of Figure 3).

As mentioned earlier, people can either develop an enduring trait-like habit of engaging in this emotional compensation (*dispositional emotional compensation*) or can employ a situationally based strategy of doing so (*situational emotional compensation*). Figure 4 depicts each form. Although situational emotional

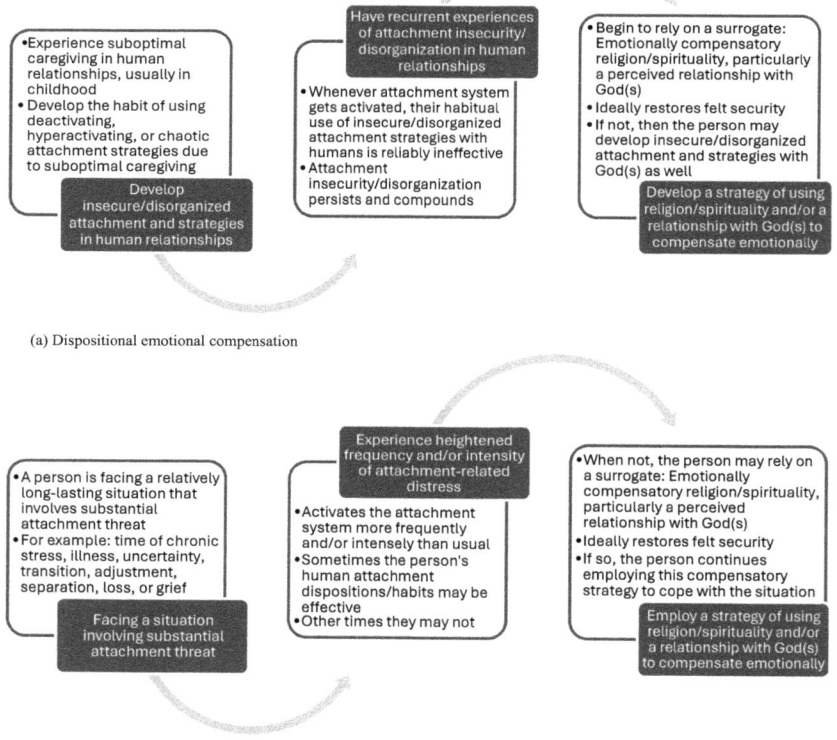

Figure 4 Two forms of the emotional compensation facet
(a) Dispositional emotional compensation
(b) Situational emotional compensation
This figure is also available to view online at
www.cambridge.org/davis-and-granqvist

compensation can occur in the case of people who have developed secure or insecure/disorganized principal attachments, dispositional emotional compensation typically occurs with people who have developed insecure (and/or disorganized) attachment and strategies in their human relationships, as was originally postulated by Kirkpatrick and Shaver (1990, 1992). Such individuals develop this enduring R/S attachment strategy to compensate emotionally for the ineffective attachment strategies/habits they developed to cope with attachment-related threat (deactivation, hyperactivation, or disorganization), based on the suboptimal caregiving they received. As we shall see, these individuals' principal insecure/ disorganized human attachment often sets the stage for a sudden, emotionally compensatory R/S conversion or intensification during adolescence or adulthood.

6.2 Research on Dispositional and Situational Emotional Compensation

6.2.1 Research on Dispositional Emotional Compensation

In research on dispositional emotional compensation, one of the most well-replicated findings is that people with an insecure childhood attachment history are especially likely to experience sudden R/S conversion or increase. This finding has been replicated cross-culturally in studies of adolescents (Granqvist, 2002; Granqvist & Hagekull, 2001, 2003) and adults (Granqvist & Hagekull, 1999; Greenwald et al., 2021; Kirkpatrick, 1997; Kirkpatrick & Shaver, 1990). Studies suggest this sudden R/S conversion or increase is particularly probable during times of transition or heightened stress, such as adolescence (Granqvist, 2002) or after a romantic breakup (Granqvist & Hagekull, 2003). It also may be more probable when the insecurely attached person was raised in a non-R/S home (Granqvist, 1998, 2005; Granqvist & Hagekull, 1999). Conversely, if an insecurely attached person was raised by highly R/S caregivers, they may be more likely to *de*convert from their caregivers' religion/spirituality (Zarzycka et al., 2024), like what Lincoln did during young adulthood (Section 5).

More broadly, research has found evidence that adolescents or adults with an insecure attachment history or disposition often develop an emotionally compensatory religion/spirituality and/or relationship with God(s). This finding has emerged with adolescents navigating a romantic breakup (Granqvist & Hagekull, 2003) and young adults who are single (Granqvist & Hagekull, 2000). It also has emerged with Israeli Jewish adults (Greenwald et al., 2021), Orthodox Jewish converts (Pirutinsky, 2009), Christian undergraduates (Kimball et al., 2013), adults who have joined new religious movements (popularly called "cults"; Buxant et al., 2010), and adults who have developed a personalized spirituality that blends traditional and nontraditional R/S beliefs and practices (Granqvist et al., 2014).

Other research indicates that adults with a principal disorganized–unresolved attachment are especially apt to report having had mystical R/S experiences during their lifetime (Granqvist et al., 2012a) and having adopted New Age R/S practices (Granqvist et al., 2007a, 2009). Mystical R/S experiences and/or New Age R/S practices may provide these individuals with an emotionally compensatory – and potentially helpful – way of framing or channeling the altered states of consciousness (e.g., dissociation/absorption) that often arise for people with a principal disorganized–disoriented/unresolved attachment (Granqvist, 2020).

6.2.2 Research on Situational Emotional Compensation

The research on situational emotional compensation focuses on more than just individuals with insecure/disorganized attachment histories or principal attachments, recognizing that all humans experience attachment threats that evoke mental/neural states of attachment insecurity for which surrogate emotional compensation may be helpful. For example, in a study of US collegiate student–athletes, Upenieks et al. (2024) found that student–athletes who were low in trait courage but had an emotionally compensatory secure R/S attachment reported lower depressive symptoms than those who reported having a less-secure R/S attachment. Likewise, in a longitudinal study of older adults who had recently lost a spouse, Brown et al. (2004) found that both securely and insecurely attached widows/widowers became more R/S over time. However, insecurely attached widows/widowers benefited the most emotionally from this increased religion/spirituality (in terms of their mental health and grief resolution), relative to their more securely attached counterparts.

Additionally, there now is robust empirical evidence that emotionally compensatory (security-enhancing) experiences in perceived relationship with God can help individuals cope with a wide range of attachment-threatening situations, many times regardless of the person's pre-existing individual differences in human or R/S attachment. Such situations include stressful contexts like postdisaster recovery (Davis et al., 2019), circumstances of socioeconomic deprivation (Liu & Froese, 2020), or situations in which people are facing heightened identity-related discrimination (Counted, 2019). There are many other situations in which emotionally compensatory experiences with God can help people cope, like when navigating stressors like a romantic breakup (Granqvist & Hagekull, 2003), the loss of a loved one (Frei-Landau et al., 2020; Kelley & Chan, 2012), the experience of a serious or chronic physical illness (Cassibba et al., 2014; Francis-Tan, 2024; Hatefi et al., 2019; Runnels et al., 2018), or the experience of a significant or persistent mental health difficulty (Diaz et al., 2010; Homan & Boyatzis, 2010; Rieben et al., 2014).

Next, we explore case examples of two historical figures who exhibited dispositional or situational emotional compensation during consequential phases of their lives.

6.3 Case Examples

6.3.1 Abraham Lincoln: Dispositional Emotional Compensation during His 40s and 50s

> "Mary, we will not return immediately to Springfield. We will go abroad among strangers where I can rest ... We will visit the Holy land and see those places hallowed by the footsteps of the Savior. There is no place I so much desire to see as Jerusalem."
> – Abraham Lincoln's last words, whispered to his wife moments before his assassination (quoted in Mansfield, 2012, p. xvii)

In Section 5, we explored the earlier phases of Lincoln's life and career, including his prolonged phase of "angry atheism." Historical accounts suggest Lincoln may have softened these R/S beliefs during the 1840s (e.g., he began reaffirming God's existence and providence), but it was ultimately a personal tragedy that catalyzed Lincoln's R/S transformation and reconversion to Christianity. In 1850, the Lincolns' 3-year-old son Edward fell ill, battled for 2 months, and died. In their grief, the Lincolns turned to a local minister who helped guide and comfort them through bereavement. They started attending this minister's church regularly, and Lincoln began a gradual process of R/S transformation and slow resocialization to his late mother's heartfelt, guiding Christian faith. Evidencing this nascent R/S transformation, in an 1851 letter Lincoln wrote to his brother upon hearing their father was dying, Lincoln shared from a seemingly forgiving, compassionate, and spiritually awakened heart: "I sincerely hope Father may yet recover his health; but at all events, tell him to remember to call upon, and confide in, our great, and good, and merciful Maker; who will not turn away from him in any extremity" (quoted in Mansfield, 2012, p. 88).

Throughout the antebellum years, Lincoln started giving generously to several churches. Since childhood, he had voraciously read the Bible (his lifelong favorite book), but he now relied on it for emotional comfort, and it became the guiding compass for his moral character and conduct. He began always keeping a Bible nearby or in his pocket, and his conversations became replete with Scripture verses, whether his hearers realized it or not. Lincoln's wife recounted his R/S transformation in an 1870 letter:

> From the time of the death of our little Edward, I believe my husband's heart, was directed towards religion & as time passed on – when Mr. Lincoln

became elevated to Office – with the care of a great Nation upon his shoulders – when devastating war was upon us – then indeed to my own knowledge – did his great heart go up daily, hourly, in prayer to God – for his sustaining power. (quoted in Mansfield, 2012, p. 86)

Lincoln's Christian faith became even more personal and experiential after the death of their son Willie, who died in 1862 at age 11. After that, Lincoln not only seems to have developed an attachment bond with God but an secure R/S attachment disposition as well. He prayed daily and fervently, making personal vows to God at pivotal points in the Civil War, and publicly calling for national days of thanksgiving and praise to God. His famous Gettysburg Address and Second Inaugural Address seem to evidence a fervent Christian faith akin to his mother's. In the latter speech, Lincoln referred to the Civil War as God's judgment against the North and South for the sin of American slavery, but he concluded with a conciliatory Christian call:

With malice toward none; with charity for all; with firmness in the right, as God gives us to see the right, let us strive on to finish the work we are in; to bind up the nation's wounds; to care for him who shall have borne the battle, and for his widow, and his orphan – to do all which may achieve and cherish a just, and a lasting peace, among ourselves, and with all nations. (quoted in Mansfield, 2012, p. 205)

6.3.2 Mother Teresa: Situational Emotional Compensation during Her "Dark Night of the Soul"

"If I ever become a Saint, I will surely be one of 'darkness.' I will continually be absent from Heaven – to light the light of those in darkness on earth."
— Mother Teresa (quoted in Kolodiejchuk, 2007, p. 1)

Saint Mother Teresa (1910–1997) grew up in a loving, close-knit, and devout Roman Catholic family, yet her childhood surroundings were marked by intense and often violent sociopolitical upheaval. Her Albanian people won short-lived autonomy from the Ottoman Empire around her second birthday, but for the next year, her people were embroiled in the Balkan Wars. For several more years, intense cultural tensions, border disputes, and political instability persisted, fueled by nationalist movements. Her father was a prominent activist in the Albanian nationalist movement, and he died when St. Teresa was 8 years old, due to suspected political assassination (Spink, 2011).

Even amid these difficult circumstances, St. Teresa seems to have developed a principal secure attachment, thanks to sensitive caregiving from both her parents. She was especially close with her mother. From early on, St. Teresa also developed a close, secure R/S attachment with God (reflecting security-based IWM correspondence). Even after her father's tragic death and her family's ensuing grief and financial instability, her mother continued instilling in St. Teresa the guiding Christian values of compassion, generosity, and kindness, particularly toward the poor, vulnerable, or marginalized. Their family prayed nightly and attended church faithfully. Love for God and neighbor and humble acts of service toward the "least of these" (Matthew 25:40) were the central elements of the Catholic religion/spirituality that St. Teresa internalized from her mother (via socialized correspondence) and eventually shared with the world.

St. Teresa felt called to a life of religious service when she was only 12, and at age 18, she left home to join the Catholic Sisters of Loreto. Due to precluding sociopolitical circumstances, she never saw her beloved mother or sister again (Kolodiejchuk, 2007; Spink, 2011).

St. Teresa continued to experience a vibrant relationship with Jesus from when she left to join the Sisters of Loreto (age 18), moved to India to start her religious training in Ignatian Catholic spirituality (age 19–21), and taught at and eventually led a Catholic school in Calcutta (age 21–38). Over those two decades, she was known privately and publicly for her compassion, kindness, cheerfulness, and dedication. However, her interior world began to shift seismically around age 36, after she discerned a call to serve "the poorest of the poor" (Kolodiejchuk, 2007, p. 44) and was released to do so at age 38. St. Teresa sensed a calling toward greater union with Christ through suffering but had no idea a half-century inner storm was brewing in her soul (Kolodiejchuk, 2007).

St. Teresa's private letters/writings were released posthumously and revealed that she experienced profound spiritual struggle, pain, darkness, and dryness from 1948 until her death in 1997. Throughout this "dark night of the soul" (St. John of the Cross, 1953/2003), St. Teresa faithfully served the poor, sick, lonely, and dying, both in India and around the globe. She founded her religious order Missionaries of Charity, which started in India, spread across the world, and gained global acclaim, and made an enormous societal impact.

Throughout her public ministry, St. Teresa served with the same cheerfulness, compassion, and vibrancy that had characterized her earlier ministry. Yet privately she struggled intensely, experiencing chronic attachment threat in her relationship with God and her religious faith more broadly. The ocean of her soul vacillated between fleeting states of R/S attachment security (which she had enjoyed throughout the first half of her life) and prolonged states of R/S attachment insecurity (which she experienced frequently during the last half of her life). St. Teresa's own words poignantly illustrate her torturous dark night. In an undated letter to Jesus, she lamented:

"Lord, my God, who am I that You should forsake me? The child of your love – and now become as the most hated one – the one You have thrown away as unwanted – unloved. I call, I cling, I want – and there is no One to answer – no One on Whom I can cling – no, No One. – Alone. The darkness is so dark – and I am alone. – Unwanted, forsaken. – The loneliness of the heart that wants love is unbearable. – Where is my faith? – even deep down, right in, there is nothing but emptiness & darkness. – My God – how painful is this unknown pain. It pains without ceasing. – I have no faith . . .

If this brings You glory, if You get a drop of joy from this – if souls are brought to You – if my suffering satiates Your Thirst – here I am Lord, with joy I accept all to the end of life – & I will smile at Your Hidden Face – always." (Kolodiejchuk, 2007, pp. 186–188)

How did Mother Teresa cope with this relentless R/S attachment insecurity and turmoil? For a while, she used hyperactivating (insecure–anxious/preoccupied) strategies, sublimating her attachment-related distress into tireless acts of service to the poor, sick, and dying. When not doing that, she micromanaged the administrative tasks of running her worldwide religious order. In her public ministry, St. Teresa was still known for being cheerful and compassionate, but privately, the sisters and staff often experienced her as exacting, irritable, and moody. This behavior may have reflected displacement of the tortuous R/S distress she felt. More adaptively, St. Teresa seems to have coped through her private communication (proximity-seeking behavior) with Jesus, the saints, her confessors, and her spiritual directors (Kolodiejchuk, 2007).

During her last two decades of her life, St. Teresa may have come to more of a place of acceptance and R/S attachment security amid her "dark night of the soul." She seems to have surrendered to Christ that this "dark night of the soul" was an expression of His love toward her and toward the precious people she loved and served. In this way, she may have regained a type of "earned" R/S attachment security that eluded her for decades of R/S turmoil (Kolodiejchuk, 2007).

6.4 Conclusion

The compensation facet described in Section 6 highlights how people may use their relationship with God(s) to compensate emotionally for states of attachment insecurity or disorganization. We argued this compensation takes two forms. First, dispositional emotional compensation denotes how individuals with insecure attachment histories or dispositions/habits develop a proclivity to turn to God(s) and religion/spirituality as attachment surrogates. Second, situational emotional compensation describes how anyone may temporarily turn to religion/spirituality during chronic circumstances that induce heightened attachment insecurity.

Our theorizing has expanded beyond the original emotional-compensation hypothesis's focus on insecurely attached individuals, based on the recognition that many people may utilize religion/spirituality for emotional compensation when human attachment figures are perceived as unavailable or unresponsive. In such a case, these people's goal is to restore felt security and deactivate the attachment system. Research on dispositional compensation indicates people with insecure attachment histories or dispositions are particularly likely to experience sudden religious conversion or intensification, especially during stressful situations and transitions. Relative to those with organized attachment dispositions, those with disorganized attachment may more frequently report mystical experiences or adopt New Age practices via a proclivity for absorption/dissociation. Research pertinent to situational compensation demonstrates that R/S attachment can help anyone, regardless of their attachment history and disposition, helping them cope with attachment-threatening situations, including spousal loss, illness, discrimination, or trauma.

Part IV Applied Theory and Research on Religious/Spiritual Attachment

7 Religious/Spiritual Attachment, Health/Well-Being, and Transformation

> *"Fortunately the human psyche, like human bones, is strongly inclined towards self-healing."*
>
> – John Bowlby (1988, p. 152)

In this concluding section, we first summarize theory and research on the relationship between R/S attachment and health/well-being (HWB). Second, we describe theory and research on whether and how positive transformation in R/S attachment security might occur, including how it may be connected to change in HWB. Third, we provide a case example illustrating how security-based interactions with human and supernatural attachment figures can promote HWB. Finally, we offer overarching Element conclusions and future research suggestions.

7.1 Foundational Theory and Research

First, conceptual clarity is needed regarding HWB and its association with religion/spirituality. According to Lomas et al.'s (2024) WHO+ framework, *health* refers to "a state of complete physical, mental, ... social [and spiritual] well-being and not merely the absence of disease or infirmity" (World Health Organization, 1946, para. 1). Likewise, according to VanderWeele and Lomas's (2023) Human Flourishing framework, *well-being* refers to "the relative attainment of a state in which all aspects of a person's life are good *as they pertain to that individual*" (VanderWeele & Lomas, 2023, p. 38). Just like religion and spirituality are highly interrelated and commonly referred to as religion/spirituality, health/well-being (HWB) are interrelated and referred to collectively as well. We focus on five facets of HWB: mental, physical, volitional, social, and R/S (Davis et al., 2026).

Importantly, contemporary theories recognize that R/S and HWB influence each other bidirectionally along four major pathways: physical pathways (e.g., genetic, epigenetic, and other biological and neurobiological influences), psychological pathways (e.g., cognitive and emotional habits and coping strategies), volitional pathways (e.g., healthy lifestyle behaviors, decision-making habits, and morally good and wise choices and behaviors), and social–environmental pathways (e.g., caregiver nurturance, family and peer influences, social support, and sociocultural and societal influences). An enormous body of evidence supports this conclusion (Davis et al., 2023, 2026; Koenig et al., 2024). Although their associations are complex, higher R/S is generally linked to higher HWB.

7.2 R/S Attachment and HWB

Theory and research on the association between R/S attachment and HWB has usually involved either (a) cross-sectional studies examining the concurrent association of the two or (b) longitudinal studies examining the effect of R/S attachment on HWB. Most of this theory/research is built on an adaptation of Section 1's Basic Principle 9. This adaptation posits that R/S attachment security (dispositional/trait or state) is concurrently and prospectively associated with higher HWB (consistent with the *broaden-and-build hypothesis of attachment security*), and R/S attachment insecurity/disorganization (dispositional/habit or state) is concurrently and prospectively associated with lower HWB (what we call the *vulnerability hypothesis of attachment insecurity/disorganization*; Cassidy & Shaver, 2016; Granqvist, 2020; Mikulincer & Shaver, 2016; Simpson et al., 2021). Here we summarize research examining these predictions, organized by the five facets of HWB. A longer summary table is available in the Element's Supplemental Material (Table S7) and at https://osf.io/dmfz3/.

7.2.1 R/S Attachment and Mental HWB

Both concurrently and prospectively, R/S attachment security has been associated with higher positive emotions, psychological well-being, life satisfaction, and trait self-esteem, as well as with lower depression, anxiety, psychological distress, and negative emotions (Almaraz et al., 2024; Bradshaw & Kent, 2018; Currier et al., 2017; Kent et al., 2018; Leman et al., 2018; Monroe & Jankowski, 2016; Stulp et al., 2019). It also has been linked to lower trait neuroticism, pessimism, and hopelessness (Ano & Pargament, 2013; Cassibba et al., 2014).

To date, there is no research on HWB's association with R/S attachment disorganization, and most research on the link between R/S attachment insecurity (anxiety and avoidance) and HWB has been cross-sectional. Both R/S attachment anxiety and avoidance have demonstrated associations with higher concurrent depression, anxiety, psychological distress, eating disorder symptoms, and nonsuicidal self-injury (Buser et al., 2020; Stulp et al., 2019). R/S attachment anxiety and avoidance are also related to (a) lower trait self-esteem and agreeableness (Rowatt & Kirkpatrick, 2002; Stulp et al., 2019); (b) higher trait neuroticism, shame, and pessimism (Ano & Pargament, 2013; Reinert, 2005); and (c) higher identity distress, body image concerns, and difficulty coping with stress/grief (Captari et al., 2021; Homan & Boyatzis, 2010).

7.2.2 R/S Attachment and Physical HWB

Few studies have examined the link between R/S attachment and physical HWB, but evidence suggests R/S attachment security is associated with healthy lifestyle behaviors (adequate sleep, nutritional eating; Almaraz et al., 2024), good sleep quality (Ellison et al., 2019), and better health-related quality of life (Counted et al., 2020). Additionally, R/S attachment security has been linked to lower levels of physical illness (Kirkpatrick & Shaver, 1992) and to anxious health preoccupation (Cassibba et al., 2014). Conversely, R/S attachment anxiety/preoccupation has been linked to more frequent dieting behavior among women (Homan & Boyatzis, 2010) and to heightened risk of obesity among adults with low social support (Krause & Hayward, 2016).

7.2.3 R/S Attachment and Volitional HWB

R/S attachment security has been linked to lower substance use (Badr et al., 2014; Hernandez et al., 2010) and to higher (a) adaptive coping behaviors (Parenteau et al., 2019), (b) positive dispositions and virtues (trait hope, optimism, compassion, humility, forgiveness, and generosity; Almaraz et al., 2024; Bradshaw & Kent, 2018; Pettit et al., 2022; Sutton et al., 2014), and (c) vocational clarity/commitment (Feenstra & Brouwer, 2008). Conversely, R/S attachment insecurity (anxious/preoccupied and avoidant/dismissing) has demonstrated associations with higher substance use (Horton et al., 2012), more dysfunctional coping behaviors (Parenteau et al., 2019), lower positive dispositions and virtues (trait self-control, self-compassion, mindfulness, forgiveness, and courage; Ghorbani et al., 2016; Sutton et al., 2014; Upenieks et al., 2024), less vocational clarity/commitment (Feenstra & Brouwer, 2008), and lower job engagement (Bickerton & Miner, 2021). R/S attachment anxiety has also been related to more inauthentic behavior and a higher propensity to accept external social influences on one's behavior (Counted & Moustafa, 2017).

7.2.4 R/S Attachment and Social HWB

R/S attachment security has been associated with (a) higher social support and lower loneliness (Almaraz et al., 2024; Ano & Pargament, 2013), (b) better social and environmental quality of life (Counted et al., 2020), and (c) stronger attachment to one's parents and family (Badr et al., 2014). Moreover, there is longitudinal evidence that R/S attachment security is linked to increased *differentiation of self* (the ability to maintain a strong sense of self and emotional connection to others, even during conflict or stress; Jankowski et al., 2022). In contrast, R/S attachment insecurity (anxiety and avoidance) has been linked to less positive relationships (Stulp et al., 2019), poorer marital adjustment/satisfaction (Knabb, 2014), lower social support, and higher loneliness (Almaraz et al., 2024; Ano & Pargament, 2013).

7.2.5 R/S Attachment and R/S HWB

Finally, R/S attachment security has been linked to several R/S HWB outcomes. For example, it is linked concurrently to higher R/S well-being, positive R/S coping, positively valenced God representations (benevolent, loving, forgiving), and R/S social support (from fellow congregants; Almaraz et al., 2024; Ano & Pargament, 2013; Cassibba et al., 2014). Longitudinal evidence suggests R/S attachment security contributes to decreased R/S struggles and increased congruence between benevolent doctrinal and experiential representations of God (Currier et al., 2024a, 2024b). Similarly, cross-sectional studies indicate that R/S attachment insecurity (anxious/preoccupied and avoidant/dismissing) is associated with (a) more negatively valenced God representations (authoritarian, judging, distant; Ano & Pargament, 2013; Bradshaw et al., 2010); (b) lower positively valenced God representations (Leman et al., 2018); (c) higher R/S struggles, instability, and disappointment (Reinert, 2005; Sandage et al., 2015); (d) lower positive R/S coping (Pirutinsky et al., 2019); and (e) greater self-directed (less God-reliant) coping (Bickerton & Miner, 2021).

7.3 Positive Transformation in Human and R/S Attachment

7.3.1 Transformation of Human Attachment

As Bowlby (1988) predicted, there is strong evidence that chronically accessible human attachment insecurity/disorganization can be transformed toward more chronically accessible attachment security. This transformation can occur via numerous avenues, typically through healthy relationships or some form(s) of intervention (psychotherapy, counseling, ministry, etc.; Mikulincer & Shaver, 2016, 2023a, 2023b; Thompson et al., 2021). Regarding the latter, there are several research-supported attachment-based interventions, including those focusing on parents–children (Attachment and Biobehavioral Catch-up; Circle of Security), families (Attachment-Focused Family Therapy), romantic couples (Emotionally Focused Couple Therapy), individual adolescents or adults (Mentalization-Based Therapy; Accelerated Experiential Dynamic Psychotherapy), or groups of adolescents or adults (Attachment-Based Group Psychotherapy). Most of these interventions are grounded in Bowlby's (1988) model of psychotherapeutic change, which suggests change in attachment dispositions/habits occurs through repeated security-enhancing interactions with attachment figures and the corresponding transformation of insecure/incoherent IWMs into more secure/coherent models (Mikulincer & Shaver, 2016).

More specifically, Bowlby (1988) argued there were five psychotherapeutic tasks involved in transforming insecure IWMs:

- Offer the person a secure base and safe haven from which to explore painful experiences from their past and current relationships, including any maladaptive beliefs/behaviors that those experiences led them to internalize about themselves, others, and relationships.
- Support the person in developing insight into how they perceive and relate with other people, especially as it involves unhelpful (and often-nonconscious) beliefs, expectations, perceptual biases, emotional reactions, and behavioral responses formed through past insecurity-enhancing relational interactions.
- Help them explore how they perceive and engage with whichever attachment figure is primarily helping facilitate transformation (psychotherapist, clergy, spouse/partner, God[s], etc.). Reflect on how identified maladaptive patterns of perceiving, thinking, feeling, expecting, and relating emerge in this relationship, affecting oneself and the relationship.
- Explore the origins and contours of maladaptive IWMs that underlie these maladaptive attachment dynamics.

- Assist the person in recognizing their maladaptive attachment representations and dispositions/habits are no longer as functionally beneficial as they were with suboptimal-caregiving attachment figures. Help them realize these unhelpful representations and dispositions/habits can be replaced by new representations and dispositions/habits that are more health-promoting (personally and interpersonally).

In short, these tasks involve psychological exploration of one's relationships with previous attachment figures, psychological and behavioral exploration of one's current relationships, and corrective experiences in relationship with at least one security-enhancing attachment figure (e.g., psychotherapist, friend, clergy, or even God[s]; Mikulincer & Shaver, 2016, 2023a, 2023b). This helps the person's attachment representations and dispositions/habits change through a process whereby the person (a) has repeated interactions with a security-enhancing attachment figure; (b) develops awareness of previously internalized mental/neural representations (of themselves, others, and relationships) that have been health-undermining in past and current relationships; (c) develops new attachment representations and dispositions/habits to replace previously internalized maladaptive ones; (d) envisions and practices new attachment representations and dispositions/habits in their current relationship(s) with the security-enhancing figure(s); and (e) internalizes those security-enhancing interactions into increasingly chronically accessible security-based representations of oneself, others, and relationships (Mikulincer & Shaver, 2004, 2016, 2023a, 2023b). Figure 5 depicts this process.

7.3.2 Transformation of R/S Attachment and Associations with HWB

There has been much less research on whether and how R/S attachment insecurity/disorganization can be changed through healthy relationships (including security-enhancing interactions with God[s]) or through psychosocial–R/S interventions. Only a dozen such studies have been published, most with significant methodological limitations.

For example, in a noncontrolled study of 99 psychiatric inpatient adults, Tisdale et al. (1997) found evidence a multimodal spiritually integrated inpatient treatment program led to positive change in patients' self-reported emotional experience of God as security-enhancing (close, loving, accepting). These adaptive changes were associated with adaptive changes in self-representations, consistent with Mikulincer and Shaver's (2004) theorizing about the formation and activation of security-based self-representations.

Another noncontrolled study of 27 outpatient adults participating in Christian-integrated individual psychotherapy yielded similar results.

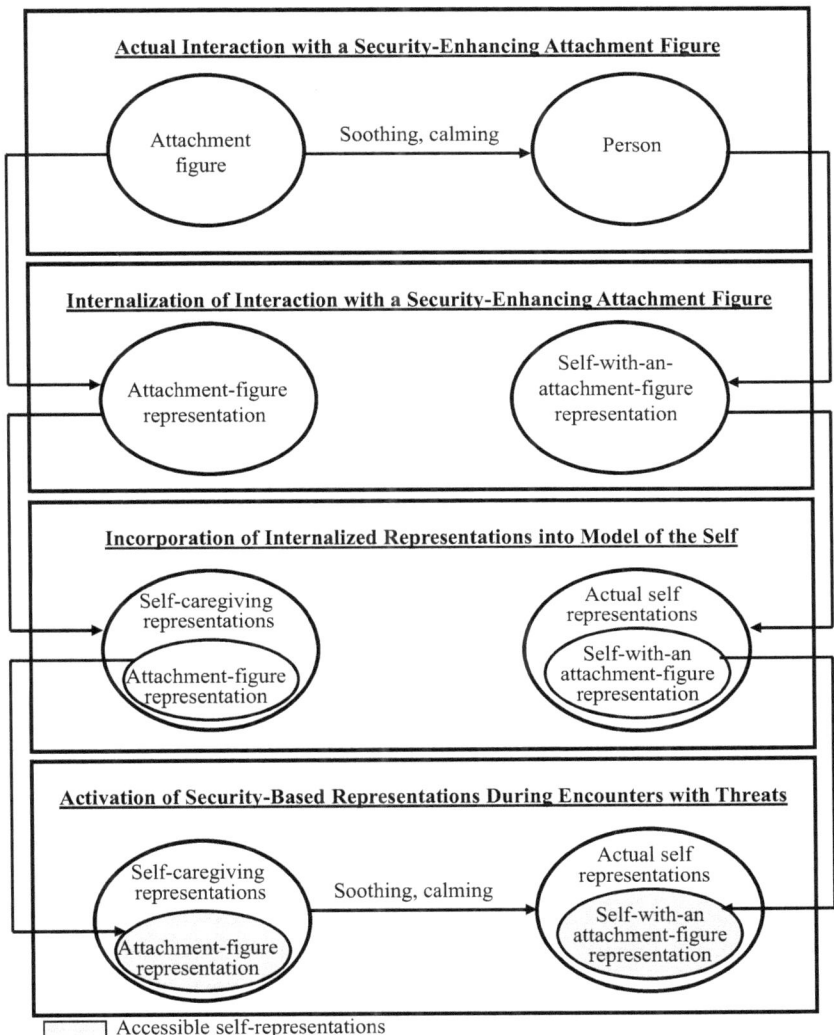

Figure 5 *The Formation and Activation of Security-Based Self-Representations* Reprinted from *Adult Attachment: Theory, Research, and Clinical Implications* (p. 186), edited by W. Steven Rholes and Jeffry Simpson, 2004, Guilford Press. Copyright 2004 by Guilford Press. Reprinted with permission.

Through in-depth behavioral and affective coding of in-session microprocesses, Kim and Chen (2022) found evidence of a 10-step rational–empirical model of therapeutic change whereby corrective emotional (security-enhancing) experiences in perceived relationship with God led to positive shifts in God representations, which in turn led to positive shifts in self-representations and consequent HWB outcomes.

In one more noncontrolled study of 26 US Christian outpatient adults, Thomas et al. (2011) found evidence a spiritually integrated group psychotherapy intervention (targeting the treatment of negative God representations) led to greater experience of God as security-enhancing. Participants reported experiencing lower R/S attachment insecurity (anxiety and avoidance) and adaptive change in their God representations (more positive/benevolent God representations, less negative/authoritarian God representations, and greater congruence between their doctrinal and experiential God representations).

As a follow-up, Rasar et al. (2013) conducted a pilot study that randomly assigned 30 US Christian undergraduates to a waitlist control group, spiritually integrated group psychotherapy intervention (the Thomas et al., 2011 protocol), or a comparable manualized group Bible study intervention. The group psychotherapy and group R/S interventions did not yield significant self-reported change in God representations or R/S attachment insecurity. However, relative to the control group, the psychotherapeutic and R/S intervention groups both evidenced significant increases in the felt love of God, self, and others (felt security from God, from oneself, and extended toward others).

In a similar controlled, nonrandomized study with 61 US Christian adults, Olson and colleagues (2016) evaluated the effectiveness of a manualized group-based R/S intervention designed to use narrative–experiential techniques to improve God representations, R/S attachment security, and narrative identity. Like the Rasar et al. (2013) study, Olson et al. (2016) found no quantitative evidence the intervention led to adaptive change in God representations or R/S attachment security. However, qualitative data from participants' postintervention journal entries and debriefing sessions told a different story. Several participants described experiencing positive psychospiritual transformation, including higher R/S attachment security, lower R/S attachment insecurity, more doctrinal–experiential congruence in their God representations, and increased self-insight and self-acceptance. The researchers pointed to the promise of using non-self-report measures of R/S attachment and God representations when conducting intervention studies (e.g., Religious Attachment Interview; God representation figure drawings).

Results from a previous study may help explain these findings. Cheston et al. (2003) conducted a controlled, nonrandomized study of general outpatient individual psychotherapy. Psychotherapy participants reported positive change in their God representations over the course of treatment (e.g., experiencing God as more agreeable/loving and less neurotic/volatile). These adaptive shifts in God representations were more pronounced among participants whose psychotherapist rated them as exhibiting high (vs. low) emotional and/or R/S change through treatment. In other words, Cheston et al. (2003) found evidence that adaptive psychotherapeutic change in psychological and R/S outcomes are associated.

Recent studies have replicated this finding. Currier et al. (2024a) conducted a noncontrolled study of 1,227 adults participating in spiritually integrated psychotherapies at practice settings in the United States (92% of clients) and other countries (8%). Patients reported significant declines in psychological distress and R/S distress, especially during the first month of treatment. Baseline levels of psychological and R/S distress were moderately correlated ($r = .42$), as were rates of decline in psychological and R/S distress ($r = .39$). Higher baseline R/S distress was linked to slower rate of decline in psychological distress ($r = .24$), but there was a strong association between higher rate of decline in R/S distress and a higher rate of decline in psychological distress. In other words, improvements in psychological HWB and R/S HWB (including R/S attachment security) were strongly and bidirectionally related. Secondary analysis of a subsample of 880 patients found that a few interventions were particularly effective in reducing psychological and/or R/S distress. For example, R/S assessment was effective in reducing both. Discussing self-control helped reduce psychological distress. Exploring R/S doubts/questions and encouraging acceptance of God's love (supporting security-enhancing interactions with God) helped reduce R/S distress.

A few other studies deserve mention. In a noncontrolled study of 241 US adults who completed a spiritually integrated inpatient program, Currier et al. (2017) found that patients evidenced adaptive shifts in their experiential representations of how God views them (reduced R/S attachment insecurity). Patients also demonstrated improvement in their R/S HWB (lower R/S struggles, higher R/S comforts) and mental HWB (lower negative emotions, higher positive emotions). One noncontrolled pilot study of a Christian-integrated residential substance use disorder program for US adult women revealed evidence of decreased R/S attachment insecurity (avoidance and anxiety) and improved mental and volitional HWB (Kerlin, 2017). Additionally, in a noncontrolled pilot study with US adults, Monroe and Jankowski (2016) found evidence a contemplative/receptive prayer intervention led to improved R/S attachment security and mental HWB, and improvements in R/S attachment security led to reduced psychological distress via increased positive emotions. Supporting the broaden-and-build theory of attachment security, boosts in felt security in perceived relationship with God led to increases in positive affect, which in turn reduced feelings of psychological distress. In one other noncontrolled study of an R/S intervention, Jankowski and colleagues (2022) found evidence a humility-focused, spiritual-formation intervention led graduate seminary students to experience improved R/S attachment security, trait humility, and differentiation of self, and these improvements were especially pronounced for students who entered the intervention with higher R/S attachment security.

Besides the US studies just reviewed, a process-based Norwegian psychodynamic therapy study ($N = 56$) found that patients' attachment behaviors toward God increased during the 3-month treatment period and remained higher than baseline at a 12-month follow-up, suggesting patients turned to God as an extension of the therapy (Halstensen et al., 2025). Intriguingly, increased attachment behaviors toward God predicted increased depressive symptoms in the early phases of treatment but also larger attenuations of depressive symptoms at treatment termination, once again highlighting the dynamic nature of connections between R/S attachment and HWB.

7.4 Case Example

7.4.1 Oprah Winfrey: Positive R/S Transformation via Sacred Relationships and R/S Attachment

American media icon Oprah was born in 1954 and spent her first 6 years raised primarily by her grandmother. Her grandmother was strict but provided well for Oprah's physical and socioemotional needs, and Oprah seems to have developed a secure attachment with her. Her grandmother's strong Baptist Christian faith was transmitted socially to Oprah. Oprah grew up going to church every Sunday, where she often recited or enacted Bible stories. She described herself as lonely during that time, growing up as an only child on their extended family's farm, but otherwise Oprah's early attachment and R/S development (and HWB) were generally positive (Kelley, 2010).

This developmental trajectory took a sharp turn at age 6, when Oprah moved to live with her mother. Oprah's mother was of low socioeconomic status and struggled to care financially and emotionally for Oprah and Oprah's half-siblings. Consequently, Oprah was often shuttled back-and-forth to live with her father and stepmother (9 hours away). Unfortunately, this caregiving instability was not the only contributor to the shift in Oprah's developmental trajectory during this period – sexual abuse and trauma were as well. Oprah was raped by a cousin at age 9, sexually molested by another relative's boyfriend from age 10 and 14, and raped by a close relative at age 14. Likely because of the latter rape, Oprah became pregnant, and her son was born very prematurely and died 5 weeks later (Kelley, 2010).

Together, these experiences of caregiving instability, poor living conditions, sexual abuse, relational trauma, stressful teenage pregnancy, and traumatic/

unresolved loss led to negative transformation in Oprah's attachment, religion/spirituality, and HWB between the ages of 6 and 15. During that period, she seems to have developed a principal disorganized–unresolved attachment with secondary avoidant–dismissing attachment. Oprah began coping by engaging in sexually promiscuous and disruptive behaviors (truancy; disobedience; argumentativeness). She also developed significant trauma-related somatic symptoms (excessive stomachaches). During this period, Although Oprah still went to Baptist church whenever living with her father, she likely experienced R/S struggles such as anger at God (Kelley, 2010).

Oprah's developmental trajectory began shifting more positively once she came to live permanently with her father at age 14. Her father was strict – presumably to overcorrect for Oprah's acting-out behavior and unstable prior home environment – but he and Oprah's stepmother provided needed stability for Oprah to improve her HWB and regain a sense of attachment security. Oprah started pouring herself into achievements. She was elected as her school's first Black student body officer, won school and state competitions for drama and public speaking, and became locally famous by doing dramatic R/S readings in Black churches (Kelley, 2010).

During her college and early professional years, Oprah struggled again in her attachment functioning and HWB, partly due to experiences of racism and sexism but partly due to resurfacing attachment insecurity and disorganization. During college, Oprah behaved quite haughtily and dismissively toward her peers, isolating herself socially. In her early 20s, she developed long-persisting habits of compulsive eating and cocaine abuse. Throughout her 20s, she had dysfunctional romantic relationships, including two affairs. And yet, positive psychospiritual transformation was brewing (Kelley, 2010).

Oprah met Gayle King at age 22, and they have been best friends for nearly 50 years. Their sacred friendship has probably been Oprah's most psychospiritually nurturing and security-enhancing attachment relationship. The mutual love, care, vulnerability, and companionship they have shared are likely the main contributor to Oprah developing an (experience) "earned" secure attachment disposition during adulthood. Gayle not only helped Oprah recover successfully from substance abuse and compulsive eating, but for decades, Gayle has helped support Oprah's HWB and personal/professional flourishing (Kelley, 2010; Winfrey, 2024).

Oprah met her long-term partner Stedman Graham in her early 30s. Their sacred partnership has also been a steadfast source of security-enhancing support. Additionally, since her early 20s, Oprah has cultivated security-enhancing relationships with close friends she considers as sacred family. These cherished souls have included Maya Angelou, Maria Shriver, Bob

Greene, Quincy Jones, and the Obamas (Kelley, 2010; Winfrey, 2024). The cast and crew of her first movie – *The Color Purple* (1985) – were similarly cherished and transformational for her. Oprah recalled their experiences as "the only time she ever felt part of a family surrounded by unconditional love .... [so] it was a spiritual evolvement for me ... I learned to love people doing that film" (Kelley, 2010, p. 127).

Lastly, Oprah has cultivated a security-enhancing R/S attachment throughout her life, but it has evolved along with her religion/spirituality. Until her mid-20s, her religion/spirituality was squarely Baptist Christian and centered on her relationship with God through Jesus Christ. Since then, her religion/spirituality has become more expansive and universalist. It still centers on connecting with a Higher Power ("God"), but the beliefs and practices she draws on to do so seem to derive from an eclectic blend of Judeo-Christian, New Age, Afrocentric, Buddhist, Hindu, and other sources. This syncretic R/S attachment has been a consistent source of security, care, comfort, and inspiration for Oprah, and she often credits God for the positive global impact of her life, work, and humanitarianism (Kelley, 2010; Taylor, 2002; Winfrey, 2024).

7.5 Section Conclusion

The first part of Section 7 summarized theoretical and empirical connections between R/S attachment and HWB. The most robust research finding is that R/S attachment security is associated with higher levels of concurrently assessed HWB, and R/S attachment insecurity is associated with lower concurrent HWB. There are relatively few longitudinal studies of the R/S attachment–HWB association. Those studies often find evidence of a prospective association between R/S attachment (in)security and subsequent HWB, but much more research is needed before firmer conclusions can be drawn. There also is a need for research on the concurrent and prospective associations between R/S attachment disorganization and HWB.

The second part of Section 7 summarized theory and research on positive transformation in human and R/S attachment, including studies examining how change in R/S attachment is associated with change in HWB. Theory and research on human attachment indicates that human attachment insecurity can be improved through the internalization of repeated security-enhancing interactions with attachment figures, whether through psychological intervention or healthy relationships (Mikulincer & Shaver, 2004, 2016, 2023a, 2023b). Although there are only a dozen published studies examining whether and how R/S attachment insecurity might be improved, those studies generally offer evidence suggesting (a) R/S attachment insecurity can be improved through psychological and/or R/S intervention, (b) adaptive change in R/S attachment security is often temporally associated with adaptive change in self-representations, and (c) these adaptive changes in R/S attachment and self-representations are associated with positive changes in HWB.

7.6 Element Conclusion

Throughout our exploration of attachment, religion, and spirituality, we have witnessed how profoundly intertwined people's relational patterns are with their R/S longings. From the conceptual foundations that established God and other supernatural figures as potential attachment figures, through the developmental trajectories that shape our capacity for transcendence, and to the attachment-related individual differences that may forecast how our R/S lives will unfold, one foundational truth emerges clearly. Humans are deeply relational beings whose search for sacred meaning and connection is inextricably woven into our search for safe, secure, and loving relationships.

The research we reviewed has revealed that people's R/S lives are neither separate from nor reducible to their psychological makeup or functioning. Instead, there is a complex dance between our attachment dispositions and our ways of seeking and responding to transcendence. Whether through correspondence (where secure attachment facilitates healthy spirituality) or compensation (where insecure attachment motivates spiritual seeking as a potential pathway to healing), our R/S experiences serve as both mirror and medicine for our relational strengths and wounds. As understanding of these dynamics grows, particularly how they apply to HWB and transformation, we are reminded that effective spiritual care and psychotherapeutic intervention should acknowledge both our psychological and R/S yearnings. The future of this field lies in bridging these domains with scientific rigor and creative ways to foster human flourishing.

The empirical literature on attachment, religion, and spirituality is still relatively nascent, especially relative to the massive literature on attachment more broadly. At this point, we suggest that future research center on a few needs. First, there is a need for more complex measurement of R/S attachment than simply self-report scales; the Religious Attachment Interview (Granqvist & Main, 2017) – developed based on the Adult Attachment Interview (Main et al., 2003) – shows particular promise but still needs robust validation. Second, there is a need for more methodologically rigorous, culturally diverse, and conceptually precise research on the correspondence facet (IWM and socialized; Section 5), the compensation facet (dispositional and situational; Section 6), and the temporal association between R/S attachment and HWB (Section 7). Third, research on religion/spirituality and attachment needs to move beyond simply the individual level; it needs to move to the level of couples, families, groups (e.g., faith communities, traditions, and subtraditions), and societies. Finally, researchers need to develop, refine, and validate interventions that can help people with prominent R/S attachment insecurity/disorganization "earn" R/S attachment security through transformative security-enhancing interactions with God(s) and other humans. Together, these research priorities will not only advance scientific understanding, but will substantially benefit people's lives, relationships, and communities. After all, religion/spirituality and attachment relationships are two of the most psychologically powerful forces in the known universe, so their science-informed union holds endless potentialities.

References

Abreu, T., Araújo, L., & Ribeiro, O. (2023). Religious factors and gerotranscendence in later life. *Current Psychology, 42*, 13938–13950. https://doi.org/10.1007/s12144-022-02706-x.

Abu-Rayya, M., Walker, R., White, F., & Abu-Rayya, H. (2016). Cultural identification and religious identification contribute differentially to the adaptation of Australian adolescent Muslims. *International Journal of Intercultural Relations, 54*, 21–33. https://doi.org/10.1016/j.ijintrel.2016.07.002.

Ai, A., Bjorck, J., Appel, H., & Huang, B. (2013). Asian American spirituality and religion. In K. Pargament, J. Exline, & J. Jones (Eds.), *APA handbook of psychology, religion, and spirituality* (Vol. 1, pp. 581–598). APA. https://doi.org/10.1037/14045-032.

Ainsworth, M. (1985). Attachments across the lifespan. *Bulletin of the New York Academy of Medicine, 61*(9), 792–812.

Ainsworth, M. (1989). Attachments beyond infancy. *American Psychologist, 44*(4), 709–716.

Ainsworth, M., Blehar, M., Waters, E., & Wall, S. (1978). *Patterns of attachment*. Lawrence Erlbaum.

Almaraz, D., Saiz, J., Baumann, K., & Moreno Martín, F. (2024). The role of spiritual well-being in Spanish cancer patients. *International Journal for the Psychology of Religion, 34*(3–4), 154–171. https://doi.org/10.1080/10508619.2024.2424612.

Angelou, M. (1978). *And still I rise*. Random House.

Anne Frank House. (n.d.). *Anne Frank*. www.annefrank.org/en/anne-frank/.

Anne Frank House. (2025). Anne Frank, her diary, and the Secret Annex. https://www.annefrank.org/en/anne-frank/

Ano, G., & Pargament, K. (2013). Predictors of spiritual struggles. *Mental Health, Religion & Culture, 16*(4), 419–434. https://doi.org/10.1080/13674676.2012.680434.

Badr, L., Taha, A., & Dee, V. (2014). Substance abuse in Middle Eastern adolescents living in two different countries. *Journal of Religion and Health, 53*(4), 1060–1074. https://doi.org/10.1007/s10943-013-9694-1.

Bakermans-Kranenburg, M., Dagan, O., Cárcamo, R., & van IJzendoorn, M. (2024). Celebrating more than 26,000 adult attachment interviews. *Attachment & Human Development, 27*(2), 191–228. https://doi.org/10.1080/14616734.2024.2422045.

Baldwin, M., Keelan, J., Fehr, B., Enns, V., & Koh-Rangarajoo, E. (1996). Social-cognitive conceptualization of attachment working models. *Journal of Personality and Social Psychology, 71*(1), 94–109. https://doi.org/10.1037/0022-3514.71.1.94.

Bartels, M. (2015). Genetics of wellbeing and its components satisfaction with life, happiness, and quality of life. *Behavior Genetics, 45*(2), 137–156. https://doi.org/10.1007/s10519-015-9713-y.

Bartholomew, K., & Horowitz, L. (1991). Attachment styles among young adults. *Journal of Personality and Social Psychology, 61*(2), 226–244. https://doi.org/10.1037/0022-3514.61.2.226.

Beck, R., & McDonald, A. (2004). Attachment to God: The Attachment to God Inventory, tests of working model correspondence, and an exploration of faith group differences. *Journal of Psychology and Theology, 32*(2), 92–103.

Bickerton, G., & Miner, M. (2021). The interrelationships between spiritual resources and work engagement. *Psychology of Religion and Spirituality, 13*(4), 448–463. https://doi.org/10.1037/rel0000253.

Birgegard, A., & Granqvist, P. (2004). The correspondence between attachment to parents and God: Three experiments using subliminal separation cues. *Personality and Social Psychology Bulletin, 30*(9), 1122–1135. https://doi.org/10.1177/0146167204264266.

Bowlby, J. (1973). *Separation: Anxiety and anger* (Vol. 2). Basic Books.

Bowlby, J. (1980). *Loss: Sadness and depression* (Vol. 3). Basic Books.

Bowlby, J. (1982). *Attachment* (Vol. 1, 2nd ed.). Basic Books. (Original work published 1969).

Bowlby, J. (1988). *A secure base*. Routledge.

Bowlby, J. (2005). *The making and breaking of affectional bonds*. Routledge. (Original work published 1979).

Bradshaw, M., Ellison, C., & Marcum, J. (2010). Attachment to God, images of God, and psychological distress in a nationwide sample of Presbyterians. *International Journal for the Psychology of Religion, 20*(2), 130–147. https://doi.org/10.1080/10508611003608049.

Bradshaw, M., & Kent, B. (2018). Prayer, attachment to God, and changes in psychological well-being in later life. *Journal of Aging and Health, 30*(5), 667–691. https://doi.org/10.1177/0898264316688116.

Brennan, K., Clark, C., & Shaver, P. (1998). Self-report measurement of adult attachment. In J. Simpson & W. Rholes (Eds.), *Attachment theory and close relationships* (pp. 46–76). Guilford Press.

Brown, M. (2017). *Frida Kahlo and her animalitos*. www.youtube.com/watch?v=gww1nyEKElo.

Brown, S., Nesse, R., & House, J., & Utz, R. (2004). Religion and emotional compensation: Results from a prospective study of widowhood. *Personality and Social Psychology Bulletin*, *30*(9), 1165–1174. https://doi.org/10.1177/014616720426375.

Buser, J., Buser, T., & Pertuit, T. (2020). Nonsuicidal self-injury and attachment to god or a higher power. *Counseling and Values*, *65*(1), 75–94. https://doi.org/10.1002/cvj.12123.

Buxant, C., Saroglou, V., & Tesser, M. (2010). Free-lance spiritual seekers. *Mental Health, Religion & Culture*, *13*(2), 209–222. https://doi.org/10.1080/13674670903334660.

Captari, L., Riggs, S., & Stephen, K. (2021). Attachment processes following traumatic loss. *Psychological Trauma*, *13*(1), 94–103. https://doi.org/10.1037/tra0000555.

Carlston, D. (2010). Models of implicit and explicit mental representation. In B. Gawronski & B. Payne (Eds.), *Handbook of implicit social cognition* (pp. 38–61). Guilford Press.

Cassibba, R., Granqvist, P., & Costantini, A. (2013). Mothers' attachment security predicts their children's sense of God's closeness. *Attachment & Human Development*, *15*(1), 51–64. https://doi.org/10.1080/14616734.2013.743253.

Cassibba, R., Granqvist, P., Costantini, A., & Gatto, S. (2008). Attachment and God representations among lay Catholics, priests, and religious. *Developmental Psychology*, *44*(6), 1753–1763. https://doi.org/10.1037/a0013772.

Cassibba, R., Papagna, S., Calabrese, M. et al. (2014). The role of attachment to God in secular and religious/spiritual ways of coping with a serious disease. *Mental Health, Religion & Culture*, *17*(3), 252–261. https://doi.org/10.1080/13674676.2013.795138.

Cassidy, J., & Shaver, P. (Eds.). (2016). *Handbook of attachment* (3rd ed.). Guilford Press.

Chamorro-Premuzic, T., von Stumm, S., & Furnham, A. (Eds.). (2015). *Wiley-Blackwell handbook of individual differences*. Wiley.

Cheston, S., Piedmont, R., Eanes, B., & Lavin, L. (2003). Changes in clients' images of God over the course of outpatient therapy. *Counseling & Values*, *47*, 96–108. https://doi.org/10.1002/j.2161-007X.2003.tb00227.x.

Codato, M., Shaver, P., Testoni, I., & Ronconi, L. (2011). Civic and moral disengagement, weak personal beliefs and unhappiness. *Testing, Psychometrics, and Methodology in Applied Psychology*, *18*(2), 87–97.

Counted, V. (2019). The role of spirituality in promoting sense of place among foreigners of African background in the Netherlands. *Ecopsychology, 11*(2), 101–109. https://doi.org/10.1089/eco.2018.0070.

Counted, V., & Moustafa, A. (2017). Between God and self: Exploring the attachment to God and authenticity/inauthenticity tendencies of South African Christian youths. *Mental Health, Religion & Culture, 20*(2), 109–127. https://doi.org/10.1080/13674676.2017.1326476.

Counted, V., Possamai, A., McAuliffe, C., & Meade, T. (2020). Attachment to Australia, attachment to God, and quality of life outcomes among African Christian diasporas in New South Wales. *Journal of Spirituality in Mental Health, 22*(1), 65–95. https://doi.org/10.1080/19349637.2018.1499165.

Cozolino, L. (2024). *The neuroscience of psychotherapy* (4th ed.). Norton.

Currier, J., Foster, J., Abernethy, A. et al. (2017). God imagery and affective outcomes in a spiritually integrative inpatient program. *Psychiatry Research, 254*, 317–322. https://doi.org/10.1016/j.psychres.2017.05.003.

Currier, J., McDermott, R., Sanders, P. et al. (2024a). Practice-based evidence for spiritually integrated psychotherapies. *Journal of Counseling Psychology, 71*(4), 291–303. https://doi.org/10.1037/cou0000727.

Currier, J., Stevens, L., McDermott, R. et al. (2024b). Exploring the roles of god representations in spiritual struggles among Christians seeking spiritually integrated psychotherapies. *Spirituality in Clinical Practice, 11*(2), 160–172. https://doi.org/10.1037/scp0000302.

Davis, E. B., Chen, Z. J., Cowden, R. G., VanderWeele, T., Oberg, S., Bivins, G., Newcity, C., Song, E., & Koenig, H. G. (2026). An overview of systematic reviews and meta-analyses on the association between religion/spirituality and health/well-being. In J. R. Webb (Ed.), Handbook of spirituality, health, and well-being: A psychological perspective (pp. 380-395). Routledge. https://doi.org/10.4324/9781003440048-25

Davis, E., Day, J., Lindia, P., & Lemke, A. (2023). Religious/spiritual development and positive psychology. In E. Davis, E. L. Worthington, & S. Schnitker (Eds.), *Handbook of positive psychology, religion, and spirituality* (pp. 279–295). Springer Nature. https://doi.org/10.1007/978-3-031-10274-5_18.

Davis, E., Granqvist, P., & Sharp, C. (2021). Theistic relational spirituality: Development, dynamics, health, and transformation. *Psychology of Religion and Spirituality, 13*(4), 401–415. https://doi.org/10.1037/rel0000219.

Davis, E., Kimball, C., Aten, J. et al. (2019). Religious meaning making and attachment in a disaster context. *Journal of Positive Psychology, 14*(5), 659–671. https://doi.org/10.1080/17439760.2018.1519592.

Davis, E., Moriarty, G., & Mauch, J. (2013). God images and god concepts. *Psychology of Religion and Spirituality*, *5*(1), 51–60. https://doi.org/10.1037/a0029289.

de Roos, S., Ledema, J., & Miedema, S. (2003). Effects of mothers' and schools' religious denomination on preschool children's God concepts. *Journal of Beliefs and Values*, *24*(2), 165–181. https://doi.org/10.1080/13617670305427.

Diaz, N., Horton, E., McIlveen, J., Weiner, M., & Williams, L. B. (2011). Spirituality, religiosity and depressive symptoms among individuals in substance-abuse treatment. *Journal of Religion & Spirituality in Social Work*, *30*(1), 71–87. https://doi.org/10.1080/15426432.2011.542729.

Douglass, F. (n.d.). *Attributed quote*: "It is easier to build strong children than to repair broken men."

Dugan, K., Kunkel, J., Fraley, R. et al. (2025). Genetic and environmental contributions to adult attachment styles. *Journal of Personality and Social Psychology*, *128*(3), 639–669. https://doi.org/10.1037/pspp0000516.

Ellison, C., Deangelis, R., Hill, T., & Froese, P. (2019). Sleep quality and the stress-buffering role of religious involvement. *Journal for the Scientific Study of Religion*, *58*(1), 251–268. https://doi.org/10.1111/jssr.12581.

Erikson, E. (1980). *Identity and the life cycle*. Norton. (Original work published 1959).

Erikson, E. H. (1994). *Identity and the life cycle*. W. W. Norton. (Original work published 1959).

Erkoreka, L., Zumarraga, M., Arrue, A. et al. (2021). Genetics of adult attachment. *World Journal of Psychiatry*, *11*(9), 530–542. https://doi.org/10.5498/wjp.v11.i9.530.

Eshleman, A., Dickie, J., Merasco, D., Shepard, A., & Johnson, M. (1999). Mother God, Father God: Children's perceptions of God's distance. *International Journal for the Psychology of Religion*, *9*(2), 139–146. https://doi.org/10.1207/s15327582ijpr0902_4.

Esfandiari, S. (2025, May 14). Artists' pets: Frida Kahlo. https://artmejo.com/artists-pets/.

Fearon, P., Schmueli-Goetz, Y., Viding, E., Fonagy, P., & Plomin, R. (2014). Genetic and environmental influences on adolescent attachment. *Journal of Child Psychology and Psychiatry*, *55*(9), 1033–1041. https://doi.org/10.1111/jcpp.12171.

Feeney, J. (2004). Transfer of attachment from parents to romantic partners. *Journal of Family Studies*, *10*(2), 220–238. https://doi.org/10.5172/jfs.327.10.2.220.

Feenstra, J., & Brouwer, A. (2008). Christian vocation: Defining relations with identity status, college adjustment, and spirituality. *Journal of Psychology & Theology, 36*, 83–93.

Fincham, F., May, R., & Kamble, S. (2019). Are Hindu representations of the divine prototypically structured? *Psychology of Religion and Spirituality, 11*(2), 101–110. https://doi.org/10.1037/rel0000166.

Fonagy, P., Gergely, G., Jurist, E., & Target, M. (2002). *Affect regulation, mentalization, and the development of the self.* Other Press.

Forslund, T., Granqvist, P., Van IJzendoorn, M. et al. (2022). Attachment goes to court: Child protection and custody issues. *Attachment & Human Development, 24*(1), 1–52. https://doi.org/10.1080/14616734.2020.1840762.

Fowler, J. (1987). *Faith development and pastoral care.* Fortress Press.

Fraley, R. (2002). Attachment stability from infancy to adulthood. *Personality and Social Psychology Review, 6*(2), 123–151. https://doi.org/10.1207/S15327957PSPR0602_03.

Fraley, R., & Davis, K. (1997). Attachment formation and transfer in young adults' close friendships and romantic relationships. *Personal Relationships, 4*(2), 131–144. https://doi.org/10.1111/j.1475-6811.1997.tb00135.x.

Fraley, R., Heffernan, M., Vicary, A., & Brumbaugh, C. (2011). The experiences in close relationships–relationship structures questionnaire. *Psychological Assessment, 23*(3), 615–625. https://doi.org/10.1037/a0022898.

Francis-Tan, A. (2024). Hope and healing: Exploring the effect of physical illness on religiosity in a longitudinal sample of Americans. *Journal of Religion and Health.* https://doi.org/10.1007/s10943-024-02181-7.

Frank, A. (2023). *The diary of a young girl.* Jaico. (Original work published 1947).

Freeze, T., & DiTommaso, E. (2015). Attachment to God and church family. *Journal of Psychology and Christianity, 34*(1), 60–72.

Frei-Landau, R., Tuval-Mashiach, R., Silberg, T., & Hasson-Ohayon, I. (2020). Attachment to God as a mediator of the relationship between religious affiliation and adjustment to child loss. *Psychological Trauma, 12*(2), 165–174. https://doi.org/10.1037/tra0000499.

Freud, S. (1953–1974). *Standard edition of the complete psychological works of Sigmund Freud* (J. Strachey, Ed./Trans., 24 vols.). Hogarth Press.

Friedlmeier, W., & Granqvist, P. (2006). Attachment transfer among German and Swedish adolescents. *Personal Relationships, 13*(3), 261–279. https://doi.org/10.1111/j.1475-6811.2006.00117.x.

Ghorbani, N., Watson, P., Omidbeiki, M., & Chen, Z. (2016). Muslim attachments to God and the "perfect man" (*Ensān-e Kāmel*). *Psychology of Religion and Spirituality*, *8*(4), 318–329. https://doi.org/10.1037/rel0000084.

Goodman, M., Raimer-Goodman, L., Gitari, S., & Seidel, S. (2022). Spirituality as compensation for low-quality social environments in childhood among young Kenyan men. *Journal of Social Psychology*, *162*(3), 371–385. https://doi.org/10.1080/00224545.2021.1909523.

Granqvist, P. (1998). Religiousness and perceived childhood attachment: On the question of compensation or correspondence. *Journal for the Scientific Study of Religion*, *37*(2), 350–367. https://doi.org/10.2307/1387533.

Granqvist, P. (2002). Attachment and religiosity in adolescence: Cross-sectional and longitudinal evaluations. *Personality and Social Psychology Bulletin*, *28*(2), 260–270. https://doi.org/10.1177/0146167202282011.

Granqvist, P. (2005). Building a bridge between attachment and religious coping: Tests of moderators and mediators. *Mental Health, Religion & Culture*, *8*(1), 35–47. https://doi.org/10.1080/13674670410001666598.

Granqvist, P. (2016). Observations of disorganized behaviour yield no magic wand. *Attachment & Human Development*, *18*(6), 529–533. https://doi.org/10.1080/14616734.2016.1189994.

Granqvist, P. (2020). *Attachment and religion: A wider view*. Guilford Press.

Granqvist, P., Broberg, A. G., & Hagekull, B. (2014). Attachment, religiousness, and distress among the religious and spiritual: Links between religious syncretism and compensation. *Mental Health, Religion & Culture*, *17*(7), 726–740. https://doi.org/10.1080/13674676.2014.906394.

Granqvist, P., Fransson, M., & Hagekull, B. (2009). Disorganized attachment, absorption, and new age spirituality. *Attachment & Human Development*, *11*(4), 385–403. https://doi.org/10.1080/14616730903016995.

Granqvist, P., & Hagekull, B. (1999). Religiousness and perceived childhood attachment: Profiling socialized correspondence and emotional compensation. *Journal for the Scientific Study of Religion*, *38*(2), 254–273. https://doi.org/10.2307/1387793.

Granqvist, P., & Hagekull, B. (2000). Religiosity, adult attachment, and why "singles" are more religious. *International Journal for the Psychology of Religion*, *10*(2), 111–123. https://doi.org/10.1207/S15327582IJPR1002_04.

Granqvist, P., & Hagekull, B. (2001). Seeking security in the new age. *Journal for the Scientific Study of Religion*, *40*(3), 527–545. https://doi.org/10.1111/0021-8294.00075.

Granqvist, P., & Hagekull, B. (2003). Longitudinal predictions of religious change in adolescence: Contributions from the interaction of attachment and relationship status. *Journal of Social and Personal Relationships*, *20*(6), 793–817. https://doi.org/10.1177/0265407503206005.

Granqvist, P., Hagekull, B., & Ivarsson, T. (2012a). Disorganized attachment promotes mystical experiences via a propensity for alterations in consciousness (absorption). *International Journal for the Psychology of Religion*, *22* (3), 180–197. https://doi.org/10.1080/10508619.2012.670012.

Granqvist, P., Ivarsson, T., Broberg, A., & Hagekull, B. (2007a). Examining relations among attachment, religiosity, and new age spirituality using the Adult Attachment Interview. *Developmental Psychology*, *43*(3), 590–601. https://doi.org/10.1037/0012-1649.43.3.590.

Granqvist, P., & Kirkpatrick, L. (2016). Attachment and religious representations and behavior. In J. Cassidy & P. Shaver (Eds.), *Handbook of attachment* (3rd ed., pp. 856–878). Guilford Press.

Granqvist, P., Ljungdahl, C., & Dickie, J. (2007b). God is nowhere, God is now here: Attachment activation, security of attachment, and perceived closeness to God among 5–7-year-old children from religious and non-religious homes. *Attachment & Human Development*, *9*, 55–71. https://doi.org/10.1080/14616730601151458.

Granqvist, P., & Main, M. (2017). *The Religious Attachment Interview: Interview questions, coding, and classification system* [Unpublished test and scoring/classification system]. Stockholm University.

Granqvist, P., Mikulincer, M., Gewirtz, V., & Shaver, P. (2012b). Experimental findings on God as an attachment figure: Normative processes and moderating effects of internal working models. *Journal of Personality and Social Psychology*, *103*(5), 804–818. https://doi.org/10.1037/a0029344.

Granqvist, P., Sroufe, L. A., Dozier, M. et al. (2017). Disorganized attachment in infancy: A review of the phenomenon and its implications for clinicians and policymakers. *Attachment & Human Development*, *19*(6), 534–558. https://doi.org/10.1080/14616734.2017.1354040.

Greenwald, Y., Mikulincer, M., Granqvist, P., & Shaver, P. (2021). Apostasy and conversion: Attachment orientations and individual differences in the process of religious change. *Psychology of Religion and Spirituality*, *13*(4), 425–436. https://doi.org/10.1037/rel0000239.

Groh, A., Roisman, G., Booth-LaForce, C. et al. (2014). Stability of attachment security from infancy to late adolescence. In C. Booth-LaForce & G. Roisman (Eds.), *The Adult Attachment Interview. Monographs of the Society for Research in Child Development*, *79*(3), 51–66. https://doi.org/10.1111/mono.12113.

Grusec, J., & Hastings, P. (Eds.). (2015). *Handbook of socialization* (2nd ed.). Guilford Press.

Hall, T., Fujikawa, A., Halcrow, S., Hill, P., & Delaney, H. (2009). Attachment to God and implicit spirituality. *Journal of Psychology and Theology, 37*(4), 227–242.

Halstensen, K., Gjestad, R., Wampold, B. et al. (2025). Addressing patients' relationships with God in psychotherapy. *Spirituality in Clinical Practice, 12* (1), 85–97. https://doi.org/10.1037/scp0000309.

Hartup, W. (1996). The company they keep: Friendships and their developmental significance. *Child Development, 67*(1), 1–13. https://doi.org/10.2307/1131681.

Hatefi, M., Tarjoman, A., & Borji, M. (2019). Do religious coping and attachment to God affect perceived pain? Study of the elderly with chronic back pain in Iran. *Journal of Religion and Health, 58*, 465–475. https://doi.org/10.1007/s10943-018-00756-9.

Hernandez, G., Salerno, J., & Bottoms, B. (2010). Attachment to God, spiritual coping, and alcohol use. *International Journal for the Psychology of Religion, 20*(2), 97–108. https://doi.org/10.1080/10508611003607983.

Herrera, H. (1983). *Frida*. Harper & Row.

Homan, K., & Boyatzis, C. (2010). The protective role of attachment to God against eating disorder risk factors. *Eating Disorders, 18*(3), 239–258. https://doi.org/10.1080/10640261003719534.

Hood, R., Hill, P., & Spilka, B. (2018). *The psychology of religion: An empirical approach* (5th ed.). Guilford Press.

Horton, K., Ellison, C., Loukas, A., Downey, D., & Barrett, J. (2012). Examining attachment to God and health risk-taking behaviors in college students. *Journal of Religion and Health, 51*(2), 552–566. https://doi.org/10.1007/s10943-010-9380-5.

James, W. (1902). *Varieties of religious experience*. Kindle Edition.

Jankowski, P., Sandage, S., Ruffing, E. et al. (2022). A mixed-method intervention study on relational spirituality and humility among religious leaders. *Spirituality in Clinical Practice, 9*(2), 87–102. https://doi.org/10.1037/scp0000248.

John, O., & Robins, R. (2021). *Handbook of personality* (4th ed.). Guilford Press.

Johnson, K., Sharp, C., Okun, M., Shariff, A., & Cohen, A. (2018). SBNR identity. *International Journal for the Psychology of Religion, 28*(2), 121–140. https://doi.org/10.1080/10508619.2018.1445893.

Jung, J. (2020). Belief in supernatural evil and mental health: Do secure attachment to God and gender matter? *Journal for the Scientific Study of Religion, 59*(1), 141–160. https://doi.org/10.1111/jssr.12645.

Kaplan, K., Dolev-Blitental, S., Galatzer, T., & Cantz, P. (2012). Individuation and attachment in Israel and Thailand: Secular versus religious Jews and Buddhists. *International Journal for the Psychology of Religion, 22*(2), 93–105. https://doi.org/10.1080/10508619.2011.646561.

Katznelson, H. (2014). Reflective functioning. *Clinical Psychology Review, 34*(2), 107–117. https://doi.org/10.1016/j.cpr.2013.12.003.

Kelley, K. (2010). *Oprah: A biography*. Random House.

Kelley, M., & Chan, K. (2012). Assessing the role of attachment to God, meaning, and religious coping as mediators in the grief experience. *Death Studies, 36*(3), 199–227. https://doi.org/10.1080/07481187.2011.553317.

Kent, B., Bradshaw, M., & Uecker, J. (2018). Forgiveness, attachment to God, and mental health outcomes in older U.S. adults. *Research on Aging, 40*(5), 456–479. https://doi.org/10.1177/0164027517706984.

Kerlin, A. (2017). Therapeutic change in a Christian SUD program. *Alcoholism Treatment Quarterly, 35*, 395–411.

Kim, E., & Chen, E. (2022). Task analysis of a Christian-integrated psychotherapy framework. *Psychotherapy, 59*(3), 363–373. https://doi.org/10.1037/pst0000406.

Kimball, C., Boyatzis, C., Cook, K., Leonard, K., & Flanagan, K. (2013). Attachment to God: A qualitative exploration of emerging adults' spiritual relationship with God. *Journal of Psychology and Theology, 41*(3), 175–188.

Kim-Spoon, J., Longo, G., & McCullough, M. (2012). Parent-adolescent relationship quality as a moderator for the influences of parents' religiousness on adolescents' religiousness and adjustment. *Journal of Youth and Adolescence, 41*(12), 1576–1587. https://doi.org/10.1007/s10964-012-9796-1.

Kıraç, F. (2021). The mediating role of self-esteem in the relationship between childhood maltreatment and god image among Turkish Muslims. *Archive for the Psychology of Religion, 43*(3), 297–316. https://doi.org/10.1177/00846724211047274.

Kirkpatrick, L. (1992). An attachment-theory approach to the psychology of religion. *International Journal for the Psychology of Religion, 2*(1), 3–28. https://doi.org/10.1207/s15327582ijpr0201_2.

Kirkpatrick, L. (1997). A longitudinal study of changes in religious belief and behavior as a function of individual differences in adult attachment style. *Journal for the Scientific Study of Religion, 36*(2), 207–217. https://doi.org/10.2307/1387553.

Kirkpatrick, L. (1998). God as a substitute attachment figure: A longitudinal study of adult attachment style and religious change in college students.

Personality and Social Psychology Bulletin, 24(9), 961–973. https://doi.org/10.1177/0146167298249004.

Kirkpatrick, L. (2005). *Attachment, evolution, and the psychology of religion.* Guilford Press.

Kirkpatrick, L., & Shaver, P. (1990). Attachment theory and religion: Childhood attachments, religious beliefs, and conversion. *Journal for the Scientific Study of Religion, 29*(3), 315–334. https://doi.org/10.2307/1386461.

Kirkpatrick, L., & Shaver, P. (1992). An attachment-theoretical approach to romantic love and religious belief. *Personality and Social Psychology Bulletin, 18*(3), 266–275. https://doi.org/10.1177/0146167292183002.

Klohnen, E., Weller, J., Luo, S., & Choe, M. (2005). Organization and predictive power of general and relationship-specific attachment models. *Personality and Social Psychology Bulletin, 31*(12), 1665–1682. https://doi.org/10.1177/0146167205278307.

Knabb, J. (2014). A preliminary investigation of the relationship between religion and marital adjustment among Christian adults from a conservative denomination. *Journal of Psychology and Christianity, 33*(3), 263–276.

Koenig, H., VanderWeele, T., & Peteet, J. (2024). *Handbook of religion and health* (3rd ed.). Oxford University Press. https://doi.org/10.1093/oso/9780190088859.001.0001.

Kolodiejchuk, B. (Ed.). (2007). *Mother Teresa: Come be my light, the private writings of the Saint of Calcutta.* Doubleday.

Krause, N., & Hayward, R. (2016). Anxious attachment to God, spiritual support, and obesity. *Journal for the Scientific Study of Religion, 55*(3), 485–497. https://doi.org/10.1111/jssr.12284.

Kübler-Ross, E. (1969). *On death and dying.* Macmillan.

Kupor, D., Laurin, K., & Levav, J. (2015). Anticipating divine protection? Reminders of god can increase nonmoral risk taking. *Psychological Science, 26*(4), 374–384. https://doi.org/10.1177/0956797614563108.

Lehmivaara, J., & Granqvist, P. (2025). Attachment and socialized religion within the Læstadian revival movement. *Nordic Psychology, 77*(1), 53–72. https://doi.org/10.1080/19012276.2023.2258558.

Leman, J., Hunter, W., Fergus, T., & Rowatt, W. (2018). Secure attachment to God uniquely linked to psychological health in a national, random sample of American adults. *International Journal for the Psychology of Religion, 28*(3), 162–173. https://doi.org/10.1080/10508619.2018.1477401.

Lerner, R., & Steinberg, L. (Eds.). (2009). *Handbook of adolescent psychology* (3rd ed.). Wiley.

Lewis, F. (2000). *Rumi.* Oneworld Publications.

Liu, Y., & Froese, P. (2020). Faith and agency: The relationships between sense of control, socioeconomic status, and beliefs about God. *Journal for the Scientific Study of Religion*, *59*(2), 311–326. https://doi.org/10.1111/jssr.12655.

Lomas, T., Pawelski, J. O., & VanderWeele, T. J. (2024). A flexible map of flourishing: The dynamics and drivers of flourishing, well-being, health, and happiness. *International Journal of Wellbeing*, 13(4), 3665. 1–38. https://doi.org/10.5502/ijw.v13i4.3665

Madigan, S., Fearon, R., van IJzendoorn, M. et al. (2023). The first 20,000 strange situation procedures: A meta-analytic review. *Psychological Bulletin*, *149*(1–2), 99–132. https://doi.org/10.1037/bul0000388.

Mahoney, A. (2010). Religion in families, 1999–2009: A relational spirituality framework. *Journal of Marriage and Family*, *72*(4), 805–827. https://doi.org/10.1111/j.1741-3737.2010.00732.x.

Maimon, D., & Kuhl, D. (2008). Social control and youth suicidality. *American Sociological Review*, *73*(6), 921–943. https://doi.org/10.1177/000312240807300603.

Main, M. (1990). Cross-cultural studies of attachment organization. *Human Development*, *33*(1), 48–61. https://doi.org/10.1159/000276502.

Main, M., Goldwyn, R., & Hesse, E. (2003). *Adult attachment scoring and classification system*. Unpublished manuscript, University of California at Berkeley, Berkeley, CA.

Main, M., & Solomon, J. (1990). Procedures for identifying infants as disorganized/disoriented during the Ainsworth Strange Situation. In M. Greenberg, D. Cicchetti, & E. Cummings (Eds.), *Attachment in the preschool years* (pp. 121–160). University of Chicago Press.

Mansfield, S. (2012). *Lincoln's battle with God*. Thomas Nelson.

McAdams, D. (2021). Narrative identity and the life story. In O. John & R. Robins (Eds.), *Handbook of personality* (4th ed., pp. 122–141). Guilford Press.

Mikulincer, M., & Shaver, P. (2004). Security-based self-representations in adulthood. In W. Rholes & J. Simpson (Eds.), *Adult attachment* (pp. 159–195). Guilford Press.

Mikulincer, M., & Shaver, P. (2016). *Attachment in adulthood* (2nd ed.). Guilford Press.

Mikulincer, M., & Shaver, P. (2023a). *Attachment theory expanded*. Guilford Press.

Mikulincer, M., & Shaver, P. (2023b). *Attachment theory applied*. Guilford Press.

Mikulincer, M., Shaver, P., & Pereg, D. (2003). Attachment theory and affect regulation. *Motivation and Emotion*, *27*(2), 77–102. https://doi.org/10.1023/A:1024515519160.

Monroe, N., & Jankowski, P. (2016). The effectiveness of a prayer intervention in promoting change in perceived attachment to God, positive affect, and psychological distress. *Spirituality in Clinical Practice*, *3*(4), 237–249. https://doi.org/10.1037/scp0000117.

Mõttus, R., Kandler, C., Luciano, M. et al. (2025). Familial similarity and heritability of personality traits and life satisfaction are higher than shown in typical single-method studies. *Journal of Personality and Social Psychology*, *128*(6), 1336–1354. https://doi.org/10.1037/pspp0000550.

Müller, M. (2013). *Anne Frank* (2nd ed.). Metropolitan Books.

Nelson, E., & Dannefer, D. (1992). Aged heterogeneity: Fact or fiction? *Gerontologist*, *32*(1), 17–23. https://doi.org/10.1093/geront/32.1.17.

Norenzayan, A., Shariff, A., Gervais, W. et al. (2016). The cultural evolution of prosocial religions. *Behavioral and Brain Sciences*, *39*, 1–65. https://doi.org/10.1017/S0140525X14001356.

Olson, T., Tisdale, T., Davis, E. et al. (2016). God image narrative therapy. *Spirituality in Clinical Practice*, *3*, 77–91. http://dx.doi.org/10.1037/scp0000096.

Opie, J., McIntosh, J., Esler, T. et al. (2021). Early childhood attachment stability and change: A meta-analysis. *Attachment & Human Development*, *23*(6), 897–930. https://doi.org/10.1080/14616734.2020.1800769.

Overall, N., Fletcher, G., & Friesen, M. (2003). Mapping the intimate relationship mind: Comparisons between three models of attachment representations. *Personality and Social Psychology Bulletin*, *29*(12), 1479–1493. http://dx.doi.org/10.1177/0146167203251519.

Overton, W. (2015). Processes, relations, and relational-developmental-systems. In W. Overton, P. Molenaar, & R. Lerner (Eds.), *Handbook of child psychology and developmental science* (7th ed., pp. 9–62). Wiley. https://doi.org/10.1002/9781118963418.childpsy102.

Parenteau, S., Hurd, K., Wu, H., & Feck, C. (2019). Attachment to God and psychological adjustment: God's responses and our coping strategies. *Journal of Religion and Health*, *58*(4), 1286–1306. https://doi.org/10.1007/s10943-019-00765-2.

Pargament, K., & Exline, J. (2022). *Working with spiritual struggles in psychotherapy*. Guilford Press.

Peterson, C., & Seligman, M. (2003). Character strengths before and after September 11. *Psychological Science*, *14*(4), 381–384. https://doi.org/10.1111/1467-9280.24482.

Pettit, R., Jin, J., Rosales, A., Fung, W., & Fung, J. (2022). The role of attachment to God in understanding religiosity and generosity among Christian young adults. *Journal of Psychology and Theology*, *50*(3), 355–368. https://doi.org/10.1177/00916471211025530.

Pew Research Center. (2012). *The global religious landscape*. www.pewresearch.org/religion/2012/12/18/global-religious-landscape-exec/.

Pew Research Center (2018). *The age gap in religion around the world*. www.pewforum.org/2018/06/13/the-age-gap-in-religion-around-the-world/.

Pew Research Center. (2020). *U.S. teens take after their parents religiously, attend services together, and enjoy family rituals*. www.pewresearch.org/religion/2020/09/10/u-s-teens-take-after-their-parents-religiously-attend-services-together-and-enjoy-family-rituals/.

Pew Research Center. (2021). *Rising share of U.S. adults are living without a spouse or partner*. www.pewresearch.org/social-trends/2021/10/05/rising-share-of-u-s-adults-are-living-without-a-spouse-or-partner/.

Pew Research Center. (2025). *2023–2024 U.S Religious Landscape Study Interactive Database*. www.pewresearch.org/religious-landscape-study/.

Pinquart, M., Feussner, C., & Ahnert, L. (2013). Meta-analytic evidence for stability in attachments from infancy to early adulthood. *Attachment & Human Development*, *15*(2), 189–218. https://doi.org/10.1080/14616734.2013.746257.

Pirutinsky, S. (2009). The terror management function of Orthodox Jewish religiosity. *Mental Health, Religion & Culture*, *12*(3), 247–256. https://doi.org/10.1080/13674670802455756.

Pirutinsky, S., Rosmarin, D., & Kirkpatrick, L. (2019). Is attachment to God a unique predictor of mental health? Test in a Jewish sample. *International Journal for the Psychology of Religion*, *29*(3), 161–171. https://doi.org/10.1080/10508619.2019.1565249.

Pollard, S., Riggs, S., & Hook, J. (2014). Mutual influences in adult romantic attachment, religious coping, and marital adjustment. *Journal of Family Psychology*, *28*(5), 615–624. https://doi.org/10.1037/a0036682.

Popper, K. (2014). *Conjectures and refutations*. Basic Books. (Original work published 1962).

Raby, K., Fraley, R., & Roisman, G. (2021). Categorical or dimensional measures of attachment? Insights from factor-analytic and taxometric research. In R. Thompson, J. Simpson, & L. Berlin (Eds.), *Attachment* (pp. 70–77). Guilford Press.

Rasar, J., Garzon, F., Volk, F., O'Hare, C., & Moriarty, G. (2013). The efficacy of a manualized group treatment protocol for changing God image, attachment to God, religious coping, and love of God, others, and self. *Journal of Psychology and Theology, 41*(4), 267–280.

Reinert, D. (2005). Spirituality, self-representations, and attachment to parents: A longitudinal study of Roman Catholic college seminarians. *Counseling and Values, 49*(3), 226–238. https://doi.org/10.1002/j.2161-007X.2005.tb01025.x.

Rieben, I., Huguelet, P., Lopes, F., Mohr, S., & Brandt, P.-Y. (2014). Attachment and spiritual coping in patients with chronic schizophrenia. *Mental Health, Religion & Culture, 17*(8), 812–826. https://doi.org/10.1080/13674676.2014.908045.

Rizzuto, A.-M. (1979). *The birth of the living God*. University of Chicago Press.

Rowatt, W., & Kirkpatrick, L. (2002). Two dimensions of attachment to God and their relation to affect, religiosity, and personality constructs. *Journal for the Scientific Study of Religion, 41*(4), 637–651. https://doi.org/10.1111/1468-5906.00143.

Runnels, R., Parker, K., & Erwin, K. (2018). Identifying spiritual markers in African American HIV positive women. *Journal of Religion & Spirituality in Social Work, 37*(4), 395–413. https://doi.org/10.1080/15426432.2018.1503070.

Ryan, R., & Deci, E. (2000). Self-determination theory and the facilitation of intrinsic motivation, social development, and well-being. *American Psychologist, 55*(1), 68–78. https://doi.org/10.1037/0003-066X.55.1.68.

St. John of the Cross. (2003). *The dark night of the soul*. Dover Publications. (Original work published 1953).

Sandage, S., Jankowski, P., Crabtree, S., & Schweer, M. (2015). Attachment to God, adult attachment, and spiritual pathology. *Mental Health, Religion & Culture, 18*(10), 795–808. https://doi.org/10.1080/13674676.2015.1090965.

Saroglou, V. (2011). Believing, bonding, behaving, and belonging: The Big Four religious dimensions and cultural variation. *Journal of Cross-Cultural Psychology, 42*(8), 1320–1340. https://doi.org/10.1177/0022022111412267.

Schnitker, S., King, P., & Houltberg, B. (2019). Religion, spirituality, and thriving: Transcendent narrative, virtue, and telos. *Journal of Research on Adolescence, 29*(2), 276–290. https://doi.org/10.1111/jora.12443.

Siegel, D. (2012). *The pocket guide to interpersonal neurobiology*. Norton.

Siegel, D. (2020). *The developing mind* (3rd ed.). Guilford Press.

Simpson, J., Rholes, W., Eller, J., & Paetzold, R. (2021). Major principles of attachment theory. In P. Van Lange, E. Higgins, & A. Kruglanski (Eds.), *Social psychology* (3rd ed., pp. 222–239). Guilford Press.

Smith, C., & Denton, M. (2009). *Soul searching: The religious and spiritual lives of American teenagers*. Oxford University Press.

Smith, E., & Kosslyn, S. (2007). *Cognitive psychology*. Pearson.

Smith, C., & Snell, P. (2009). *Souls in transition: The religious and spiritual lives of emerging adults*. Oxford University Press.

Spink, K. (2011). *Mother Teresa* (Rev. ed.). HarperCollins.

Stulp, H., Koelen, J., Schep-Akkerman, A., Glas, G. G., & Eurelings-Bontekoe, L. (2019). God representations and aspects of psychological functioning: A meta-analysis. *Cogent Psychology*, *6*(1), 1–50. https://doi.org/10.1080/23311908.2019.1647926.

Sullivan, P. F., Neale, M. C., & Kendler, K. (2000). Genetic epidemiology of major depression: Review and meta-analysis. *American Journal of Psychiatry*, *157*, 1552–1562. https://doi.org/10.1176/appi.ajp.157.10.1552.

Sutton, G., Jordan, K., & Worthington, E. L. (2014). Spirituality, hope, compassion, and forgiveness: Contributions of Pentecostal spirituality to godly love. *Journal of Psychology and Christianity*, *33*, 212–226.

Tamminen, K. (1994). Religious experiences in childhood and adolescence. *International Journal for the Psychology of Religion*, *4*(2), 61–85. https://doi.org/10.1207/s15327582ijpr0402_1.

Taylor, L. (2002, April 1). The church of O. *Christianity Today*. www.christianitytoday.com/2002/04/church-oprah-winfrey/.

Teresa, M. (1995). *A simple path*. Ballantine Books.

Thomas, M., Moriarty, G., Davis, E., & Anderson, E. (2011). The effects of a manualized group-psychotherapy intervention on client god images and attachment to God. *Journal of Psychology and Theology*, *39*, 44–58. https://doi.org/10.1177/009164711103900104.

Thompson, R., Simpson, J., & Berlin, L. (Eds.). (2021). *Attachment: The fundamental questions*. Guilford Press.

Tisdale, T., Key, T., Edwards, K. et al. (1997). Impact of treatment on God image and personal adjustment, and correlations of God image to personal adjustment and object relations development. *Journal of Psychology and Theology*, *25*(2), 227–239.

Tornstam, L. (2011). Maturing into gerotranscendence. *Journal of Transpersonal Psychology*, *43*(2), 166–180.

Upenieks, L., Bounds, E., Melton, K., Glanzer, P., & Schnitker, S. (2024). Trait courage, attachment to god, and mental well-being among U.S. collegiate athletes. *Journal of Religion and Health*, *63*(4), 2941–2962. https://doi.org/10.1007/s10943-024-02054-z.

VanderWeele, T. J., & Lomas, T. (2023). Terminology and the well-being literature. *Affective Science*, 4, 36–40. https://doi.org/10.1007/s42761-022-00153-2

van Ijzendoorn, M., & Bakermans-Kranenburg, M. (2019). Bridges across the intergenerational transmission of attachment gap. *Current Opinion in Psychology*, *25*, 31–36. https://doi.org/10.1016/j.copsyc.2018.02.014.

van IJzendoorn, M., & Bakermans-Kranenburg, M. (Eds.). (2024). *Matters of significance: Replication, translation, and academic freedom in developmental science.* UCL Press. https://doi.org/10.14324/111.9781800086500.

Van Tongeren, D. R. (2024). *Done: How to flourish after leaving religion.* APA.

Vannucci, A., Yu, W., Martin, N., Patel, S., & Tottenham, N. (2025). Affective schemas: Acquisition, updating, and inference. *Emotion.* Advance online publication. https://dx.doi.org/10.1037/emo0001561.

Verhage, M., Schuengel, C., Madigan, S. et al. (2016). Narrowing the transmission gap: A synthesis of three decades of research on intergenerational transmission of attachment. *Psychological Bulletin, 142*(4), 337–366. https://doi.org/10.1037/bul0000038.

Vonk, J., Zeigler-Hill, V., Cater, T., & Aradhye, C. (2019). Believe what I believe: Correspondence between the beliefs of young adults and the perceived beliefs of their caregivers. *Journal of Genetic Psychology, 180*(2–3), 103–113. https://doi.org/10.1080/00221325.2019.1596877.

Vukasović, T., & Bratko, D. (2015). Heritability of personality: A meta-analysis of behavior genetic studies. *Psychological Bulletin, 141*(4), 769–785. https://doi.org/10.1037/bul0000017.

Weiss, R. S. (1973). *Loneliness.* MIT Press.

Wellman, H., Cross, D., & Watson, J. (2001). Meta-analysis of theory-of-mind development. *Child Development, 72*(3), 655–684. https://doi.org/10.1111/1467-8624.00304.

White, C. (2021). *An introduction to the cognitive science of religion.* Routledge.

White, R. (2009). *A. Lincoln.* Random House.

Winnicott, D. (1992). *Through paediatrics to psycho-analysis.* Brunner-Routledge. (Original work published 1975).

Winfrey, O. (2024). *What I know for sure.* Flatiron Books.

Zarzycka, B. (2019). Parental attachment styles and religious and spiritual struggle. *Journal of Family Issues, 40*(5), 575–593. https://doi.org/10.1177/0192513X18813186.

Zarzycka, B., Grupa, M., Krok, D., & Rynasiewicz, A. (2024). Parental attachment styles, religiousness, and deconversion processes in adolescence. *Mental Health, Religion & Culture, 27*(1), 87–100. https://doi.org/10.1080/13674676.2024.2304302.

Zhang, H., Chan, D., & Teng, F. (2011). Transfer of attachment functions and adjustment among young adults in China. *Journal of Social Psychology, 151*(3), 257–273. https://doi.org/10.1080/00224545.2010.481685.

Cambridge Elements

Psychology of Religion

Jonathan Lewis-Jong
St Mary's University Twickenham and University of Oxford

Jonathan Lewis-Jong is Researcher in Psychology of Religion at the Benedict XVI Centre for Religion and Society at St Mary's University, Twickenham, and an Associate of the Ian Ramsey Centre for Science and Religion at the University of Oxford. His recent books include *Experimenting with Religion* (2023) and *Death Anxiety and Religion Belief* (2016). He is also an Associate Editor at the American Psychological Association journal *Psychology of Religion and Spirituality*.

Editorial Board

Paul Bloom, *University of Toronto*
Adam B. Cohen, *Arizona State University*
Ara Norenzayan, *University of British Columbia*
Crystal Park, *University of Connecticut*
Aiyana Willard, *Brunel University*
Jacqueline Woolley, *University of Texas at Austin*

About the Series

This series offers authoritative introductions to central topics in the psychology of religion, covering the psychological causes, consequences, and correlates of religion, as well as conceptual and methodological issues. The Elements reflect diverse perspectives, including from developmental, evolutionary, cognitive, social, personality and clinical psychology, and neuroscience.

Cambridge Elements

Psychology of Religion

Elements in the Series

Divination: A Cognitive Perspective
Ze Hong

Morality and the Gods
Benjamin Grant Purzycki

The Psychology of Mysticism
Zhuo Job Chen

Attachment, Religion, and Spirituality
Edward (Ward) B. Davis and Pehr Granqvist

A full series listing is available at: www.cambridge.org/EPOR

For EU product safety concerns, contact us at Calle de José Abascal, 56–1°, 28003 Madrid, Spain or eugpsr@cambridge.org.

www.ingramcontent.com/pod-product-compliance
Ingram Content Group UK Ltd.
Pitfield, Milton Keynes, MK11 3LW, UK
UKHW022318240426
470365UK00021B/681